Living & Dying In The

Fourth Year

Brian Neese, MD, MPH

Aventine Press

Published by Aventine Press
750 State St. #319
San Diego CA, 92101
www.aventinepress.com

ISBN: 1-59330-648-2

Library of Congress Control Number: 2010923931
Library of Congress Cataloging-in-Publication Data
Living & Dying in the Fourth Year

Printed in the United States of America

To my mother
Who says I never tell her any stories from medicine

I wish I had another life to live
Not of regret
But of insatiable curiosity

Table of Contents

Preface

Try this out sometime: go to a medical school a few months into the school year and stand at the door of a basic physiology classroom. When the first year students start pouring out, take one aside and say the words "fourth year". You will see a softening of their tense forehead lines. The bags under their sleep deprived eyes will lighten a shade. To understand this reaction is to understand the foundation of this book. Let me explain.

The United States medical school curriculum is four years long. A student arrives in the fall and is immediately labeled as a 'first year'. The year of medical study denotes in exquisite detail what occupies 90% of their wake-time. In first year, all learning occurs in the classroom with courses on how the body works, such as Anatomy, Physiology, Immunology, and Pharmacology. The second year is much of the same, with the focus on what can go wrong in the body through pathology and disease.

It is not until third year that a medical student leaves the classroom for the sterile halls of the hospital ward. While finally getting their hands on real patients, this period is marked by a constant melee of strife and confusion. Rotating through Internal Medicine, Pediatrics, Surgery, and Obstetrics is like landing on the shores of savage aboriginal land; survival is a must, but is always in question.

What happens next is the closest thing to freedom a medical student will ever know. It is fourth year. The shackles of obligatory curricula are loosened and students pursue their own electives. These courses can be done at their home institution, in another state, or even another country. If a student has travel aspirations, this is their best opportunity to have a meaningful experience abroad. At my alma mater, the Medical School for

International Health (MSIH), the fourth year is a promise to travel the world.

MSIH is a collaborative medical program between Columbia University in New York City and Ben Gurion University of the Negev in Beer Sheva, Israel. The mission is to train up competent physicians who are experts in International Health and Cross-Cultural Medicine. The method is revolutionary in scope, taking the standard four year U.S. curriculum and outfitting it with an intense, longitudinal experience in every facet of cross-cultural medicine.

Students live and study in Israel for the first three years. Classes are taught in English and follow the same schedule as U.S. schools. The patients, however, are not English speaking. Hebrew language training is required; Arabic, Russian, and others are encouraged.

Public Health courses such as Epidemiology and Biostatistics, as well as classes in Disaster Relief, International Health and Cross-Cultural communication are integrated into the regular curriculum. The capstone experience is the fourth year international clerkship where students spend two months in well developed clinical rotations in countries such as India, Kenya, Ethiopia, and Peru.

This is the mold from which I came, where my own curiosity and love of foreign cultures married into the medical profession. The fourth year was the pinnacle of this experience; a year of intense cross cultural medical training that I would gladly do over again. *Living & Dying in the Fourth Year* is my way of doing just that.

Introduction

Avner's Paradox

The room was buzzing with surgical prep activities. A grossly overweight Israeli cab driver named Avner lay still on the surgical table, perfectly centered in the operating room. His whole body was covered by mint green surgical drapes, save for his gently rising and falling chest which was being cleansed by a nurse. To the right was a large machine full of visible pipes like the tunnels of an ant farm. Technicians were prepping this bypass machine, turning knobs, and setting calibrations. There was silence in the air held together by the gravity of the act about to take place.

The nurses then hung up the drape covering Avner's massive body to obscure the view between the surgical site and his face. This measure helped everyone forget that this flesh was connected to a real human being, a life being tinkered with in a potentially grave manner.

The anesthesiologist then prepared a syringe full of a thick, white solution called propofol, or Milk of Amnesia as it is commonly known. He pushed the milky fluid through a small I.V. line in Avner's arm. He spoke in Hebrew, but with an ominous Russian accent, "Good night and good luck." The fatalistic tone of his voice inspired fear, even in me. Avner responded to this salutation, but was mid-sentence when he began snoring.

The first surgeon then entered the swinging theater doors. He held his hands in the air, elbows bent at 90 degrees as if in a strange prayer of thanksgiving. Water dripped to the floor.

After gowning up, he grabbed a saw and began his days work. With great force and effort the breastplate was sawed opened. There it was, the beating human heart, the seat of this man's soul that was now being treated like an engine transmission. The surgeon then dissected out the heart and the cardiac cavity was filled with sterile ice. The heart beat began to slow.

Tubes were then placed in the Pulmonic and Aortic arteries for transfusion. Plastic coiled cylinders exited his chest cavity pushing blood to the huge bypass machine nearby. There, it was oxygenated and pumped right back into the body. Avner Levin, the Beer Sheva cabbie, was now a pod from *The Matrix*.

The slowly beating heart was then injected with Potassium Chloride. This brought all cardiac motion to a halt. The heart lay there, quietly resting on ice as if being served at a cocktail party. I wondered how many Type-A personalities had history needed to make such a barbaric procedure a reality? How many brave volunteers were needed to perfect it?

The surgeon then folded his hands, letting them rest on the sterile field before him. The surgical techs became quiet. The anesthesiologist sat motionless staring at the monitors behind Avner's head. The deafening silence was broken only by the soft swishing sound of the coils pumping air into his lungs.

That the human being can be treated like a machine, broken down into its fundamental parts and tinkered with at will, is the great advancement of modern medicine. That we train people to do it so effectively, improving with each generation of student, is the energy behind this achievement. Yet for me standing there looking at this heart, I wanted nothing to do with the scalpel. There was a personal story, even a historical context, attached to that flesh that intrigued me far more than the organ itself.

The operating room where Avner Levin offered up his heart for my contemplation was located in Beer Sheva, Israel. I was at the end of my fourth and final year of study at the Medical School for International Health (MSIH), a collaborative M.D. program between Columbia University in New York City and Ben-Gurion University in Israel. I had spent three and a half years intensively pursuing medicine, caught for most of that time at the fulcrum of Avner's paradox between the brute mechanics of the medical profession, and the flowing, emotional art of caring for a patient. Forced to the former, I longed for the latter.

As a result, I rarely shook off the gnawing thought that I wasn't meant to be a doctor. Clearly this internal conflict would ruin my life, my career, or both. And then I embarked on my fourth year. The curriculum called for electives in the U.S.A. and Israel, and two months in a third world country for an International Health clerkship. I would travel, study, hear foreign languages, and meet people of a hundred different cultures. I would see disease present itself in ways I could not yet imagine. This fourth year journey was a path of study so unique, so provocative in its concept, and so uncomfortable in its course, that it led me to my own space in the practice of medicine. When I stood at the foot of Avner's bed, I saw the same old conflict, but in a new light and with total peace about where I belonged in this patient's life. This is the story of how I discovered the humanistic side of medicine.

New York City
E.R.

St. Luke's and Saving Arthur

The St. Luke's Hospital Emergency Department is a designated trauma center in Manhattan, and I was signed up to spend 15 of July's 31 days working 10 hour shifts there. My role as a fourth year medical student, however, was ambiguous. My orientation papers had formal statements like: *The student will perform a History and Physical on patients and assist the attending physician and the residents in the care of patients.* These conjured mental images of catching a patient gurney from the ambulance driver as it flew through the swinging ER doors.

"Let's get a line on this guy!" I would yell. "Somebody get me a liter of Normal Saline running wide open stat! Has anyone drawn up the milligram of Epi I asked for! We've got a life on the line here!"

Deep down I knew those were mere fantasies from my experience as a third year medical student. Reality was more like this: "Brian, go ask the nurse where the bedpans are and make sure Mr. Smith doesn't puke all over the EKG machine." Humbling, as always, but not unexpected for the medical student, who occupies the lowest rung on the medical hierarchy.

The St. Luke's ER sits on the corner of 113th St. and Amsterdam Ave. and is guarded on two sides. The main street entrance is flanked by an Arab guy selling muffins from a one man metal cart. I waited every morning in his long lines for $1 blueberry muffins. The side street ER entrance is guarded by the monumental Cathedral of St. John the Divine. After more than one long ER shift, I left to sit in that cavernous sanctuary. There is a sense of awe bestowed by the architecture, a foreboding purpose in every angle of its gothic stone.

Inside the ER life hummed day and night. Nurses, resident physicians, phlebotomists, and paramedics crawled like ants through the labyrinthine maze of patient bays and rooms. The energy in that atmosphere charged the chronically fatigued bodies and minds that pulled shifts day and night. At the least, time went by fast because in a New York City Emergency Room, there are always patients to be seen.

These patients are in a state of acute vulnerability. Their guard is down and far more than their pathology is exposed. Their insecurities, their faults, all the things they'd rather keep to themselves, or at least within the smallness of their personal world, are laid bare. Physicians have the first contact with this side of people. It is instant intimacy.

Arthur was a patient well known to the residents at St. Luke's. He came in regularly in a drunken stupor, looking for a bed to pass the night and some food if he was lucky. He was not well known to me, however, as he arrived during my very first shift of the rotation. The residents had a little fun at my expense.

"Hey Brian," a rosy cheeked second year resident named Dr. Fernandez called out, "we've got a patient in Bay 19, why don't you go work him up. And do everything, this one could be serious."

I was glad to see this patient. In fact, my interest could hardly be greater. Fernandez said this could be serious and I was given the chance to see the patient first. I grabbed his chart and scanned the triage note and vital signs. Throwing back the curtain to Bay 19 my eyes fell upon an old and sturdy African-American man. He wore tattered clothes, brown leather shoes without laces and a sock on his left foot only. His button up shirt was once white but corruptibly stained by years of dirty streets and subways. He snored softly and rhythmically, sleeping as peacefully as someone so disheveled could hope to sleep.

"Arthur. Arthur. Can you hear me?" I asked. "My name is Brian Neese. I am a medical student here. Hello, Arthur!" Arthur only stirred slightly, repositioning himself to continue his hard slumber.

The most important lesson imparted to young doctors-to-be is to discern a patient as Sick or Not Sick. My third year of medical school was my first and only year of clinical experience, but even I could tell that this man was Not Sick. He was sleeping with stable vital signs. I postponed the H&P in order to clarify Arthur's known history with Fernandez. I also wondered if I had been a little duped.

"Mr. Arthur, I'll be back in a second, okay?" I said.

I marched back to the nurse's station in the middle of the ER where residents worked on patient orders. Before I got a word out, I saw snickers from Fernandez and another resident, Dr. Mason.

Fernandez, with a very serious glare on his baby face, asked me, "So what do you think, Brian? Is he gonna make it?" And with that he failed to keep a straight face.

"Yeah, well, he's having a good nap. He's just drunk, isn't he?" I asked. "I guess it's not the first time he's shown up here?"

"You could set your clock by it," Mason responded. "Sorry man, we were just messing with you a little bit. This won't be the last drunk you see though, so there's your warning. We're obligated to work him up even though we know damn well he doesn't need anything but sleep and food. Do your best and let us know if you need some help."

I headed back to see Arthur, wondering if this was the most efficient use of very expensive medical care, even with me as the deliverer. But in American medical culture, there was the umbrella of CYA (Cover Your Ass) that affected every decision made. Countless dollars poured into patient care for no other indication than CYA. Arthur got the full work up, again. He would get it next month as well, perpetuating himself under the care of yet another unwitting medical student.

The biggest challenge of that H&P was keeping Arthur awake and interested enough to answer my questions. When I asked him about alcohol use, I expected an honest answer from a man so obviously intoxicated.

"Do you drink alcohol?" I asked. Arthur flippantly denied the behavior. I wondered if he really understood the question. I repeated myself, and again he said, "No, man, I don't drink!"

If he was not in such a pathetic state it would've been comical to hear this reply. I re-phrased the question and asked again, "So you're telling me, to be clear, that in all your life, a drop of alcohol has never touched your lips?"

He adjusted himself in the gurney, shifting his body into a more comfortable position, not once looking me in the eye. Casting a glance down, then up to the ceiling and forward again he said to me, "Sheeit boy, now you know I can't tell dat lie!"

I wanted to hug him for his moment of lucid honesty. What a bond was forged between us, some shared trust that he could now open up to me. This delusion was quickly shattered when he denied smoking cigarettes, showing woeful disregard for the pack of cigarettes in his breast pocket. We danced the same way until he repeated himself, "Sheeit boy, now you know I can't tell dat lie!"

The Billowing Irishman

The International Student Center Youth Hostel on Manhattan's Upper Westside was my home for the month of July. Living on student loans made finding an affordable space to lay my head nearly impossible. The Youth Hostel had beds for $25 a night, a price I could handle, and with some minor pleading they let me stay for the whole month. Any longer, though, and I'd be scrubbing toilets to earn my keep.

When I arrived at the hostel that evening after babysitting Arthur, the front desk of the hostel was being manned by a young Indian-American girl from Chicago. Her family had tried to marry her off to someone back home, so she fled to Manhattan to strike her own path. There is always a reason people end up in New York City. They are usually fleeing something from where they came and the city absorbs, like a sponge, the gold and dirt, the diamonds and the scum of the earth.

My bed was on the third floor, and one of eight in the room. There was no privacy and no barriers. Linens were provided for free, and that was good. But, the hostel prohibited travel packs in the rooms, and that was bad. In fact, of all the inconveniences for me, this was the greatest. I was allowed to bring my blue JanSport backpack with me, but my large internal-frame pack with all of my clothes and books stayed in the office area. If I got home after office hours, which happened not infrequently, I did not have access to my belongings.

Luckily I had landed a rare non-bunk bed. It was situated in the back corner under the street side window. My alarm clock for the most part was the sun and the horns of cars passing by on 88th street, near the corner of Central Park West. It was a beautiful street lined with brownstone apartments, the classic picture of Manhattan living.

I lumbered up the stairs to my dorm room and slipped through the door without waking anyone. I'd be back at the ER in the morning by the time the front office opened up with access to my pack, so I packed up my clothes and medical accessories and brought them with me upstairs. I sat on the edge of my bed in the dark room and folded my scrubs and white coat. I tucked them into the corner of the bed, above my head. On top of that I stacked my stethoscope, Maxwell's Guide, and Pocket Medicine books that stayed with me always.

In the bottom bunk of the bed facing mine, slept a man whose name I never learned. His accent was that of an Irishman. He was short and stocky, with muscles hardened by a life of manual labor. His skin was permanently stained with flecks of paint. His face was hard, and the lines on his cheek were chiseled tight and deep, but his disposition was surprisingly pleasant. He worked as a maintenance man at the hostel in exchange for his board.

As my mind drifted to the netherworld between consciousness and sleep I was aroused into cold reality by a long, wet, and gaseous fart! I immediately turned towards the sound. It was the Irishman. With the light from 88th street that made it through my plaid curtain I could see he was unaffected by his own obtrusive flatulence. He didn't even shift under his covers. I was embarrassed for having noticed, until I realized he hadn't noticed himself. Then I felt disgusted.

I suddenly felt very far from home. My wife, Shelley, was staying in our apartment four hours to the north in Boston. She was my college sweetheart, and we'd been engaged even before I was accepted to medical school. So this year of sputtering separation had been long anticipated for us both.

Still, it was only July, and 10 months separated me from finishing the year and earning the right to be called Doctor. I was scheduled to spend two months in New York City hospitals, one Emergency Medicine, the other Internal Medicine; one month in Montana working on the Crow Indian Reservation; two months in East Africa, at Moi University Hospital in Eldoret, Kenya; then I would finish with two months in Beer Sheva, Israel, where I had spent the first three years of medical school at MSIH. For now, however, I had traded my wife's long blonde hair and ocean blue eyes for the fumes of this Irish laborer.

Even these thoughts were interrupted by another echoing fart. Though not as loud as the first, it momentarily roused the Irishman. He shifted from his right to his left side, aiming to the wall instead of to me. I wanted to thank him for showing such consideration, but he was still fully asleep and fully unaware of his discomfited sleep toots.

History is 90% of the Diagnosis

The next morning, I woke up early for my next ER shift. Before leaving the hostel, I went down to the basement kitchen to make a peanut butter and jelly sandwich. The kitchen functioned under the most communal of systems. Shelves by the refrigerators and stoves were full of produce and breads and cereals, all in plastic supermarket bags with names scribbled on their sides. In all my time there, I never heard of theft of someone's food. The shared poverty of the young traveler is a powerful force in food security.

My plastic bag contained the bare necessities of life: bread, peanut butter, strawberry jelly, and Macaroni & Cheese. I made up my PB & J and only then noticed I forgot to pick up sandwich bags during my grocery run. So I wrapped the sandwich in a used-only-once white undershirt, a workaround that seemed logical in those early morning hours.

I got to the ER when my shift was scheduled to start, which meant I was five minutes late, and threw shirt and sandwich into the staff refrigerator. As I slammed the small refrigerator door closed I noticed a gruesome sight. The strawberry jelly had seeped through my white Hanes undershirt, like a blood stained t-shirt stored amongst salads and Diet Pepsi's. That does not go over well in an urban Emergency Room. Personally, it was a stark reminder of how pathetic I was without my wife. I covered the shirt with some paper towels and resolved to be more responsible, or at least buy sandwich bags pronto.

My shift that day was highlighted by Mrs. Watson, a senile elderly woman who arrived by ambulance quite against her will. She was offended at being brought in for no good reason. It was unfortunate that she had so much deterioration of her grey matter. Otherwise, I think she would've agreed emphatically with the reason for her transfer.

"Hello, Mrs. Watson, how are you doing?" I asked.

"I was doing a helluva lot better in my house." She replied. "Can you believe what they did to me? What is your name? Are you a doctor?"

"Yes ma'am, well, I'm a medical student. Why did they bring you here tonight?" I asked.

"I don't know!" She answered. "Maybe you can tell me. I was playing with the kids like I always do and the next thing you know, here I am! You know, I just love to play with the little children in my building. They come over all the time, and I take them out to the playground, and we all play in the sand. They love it you know."

While Mrs. Watson continued into her story, I started the first part of any physical examination: observation. She was a frail woman with her clothing a little unkempt. She had indeed been playing in dirt, and had not washed in a good while either. Under her finger and toenails, and striped over her arms and legs, was dried, crusted dirt.

"...my daughter never, ever wanted to go again without me..." Mrs. Watson continued.

"I'm sorry Mrs. Watson, I don't mean to interrupt, but what is all this dirt from?" I asked. "Is it from playing with those kids?"

With an all-shucks tone to her voice she replied, "Oh yeah, honey, you know those kids just adore me! They're always coming by asking me to go down to the playground...."

She cycled into the same story again, verbatim. I was bothered by something else regarding ole' Mrs. Watson, something more than her appearance or her tangential ramblings. It took a few minutes to realize she had a distinct odor about her, but I could not place it to anything in particular. I leaned in closer, pretending to examine her neck veins, but really taking a good hard whiff of her body odor. The smell was stronger, but I still could not tell where it stemmed from. It emanated from all of her.

I reached down to her wrist to check her pulse, another ploy at this point because I could think of nothing else besides the mysterious smell. I picked up her wrist and noticed the smell got stronger. The whole time Mrs. Watson went on and on about her children, the neighborhood kids, and sandboxes. Since she was lost in her story I decided to be bold and put her dirty, wrinkled fingers directly under my nose. Phew! I had found the source!

I put her hand down immediately, half because she stared at me with a distant sense of wonderment and half because the smell was caustic to my nose. With so much crusted dirt under her fingernails and over her arms and legs, and with such a powerful odor, I wondered to myself how long had it been since she had bathed herself. Even without washing for a week, dirt would not smell this way. It was fetid.

I excused myself from Mrs. Watson, who started once again about the playground, as if I had never met her. I left her room and went to the nurse's station hoping to find a resident who had more information about this old lady. I even wondered if I was again set up by the residents for entertainment purposes. Off to the side I saw the ambulance driver that brought in Mrs. Watson. He was talking with a resident. I inquired what he knew about Mrs. Watson's mental and physical state prior to arrival to the ER.

"Yeah, man," he replied. "Her neighbor called the police 'cause she wasn't answerin' her phone. They showed up, busted in, and found her layin' in her own shit. We got there a little while after that. I think she mighta been there a few days."

There was nothing like a good patient history to clarify a clinical mystery! I briskly walked to the sink and spent two minutes scrubbing my hands between each digit and under each fingernail. I left no millimeter of breathing room for the disgusting bacteria that had been lodged so innocently onto my skin. I topped it off with a few squirts of hand sanitizer. In my years of medical training, I had never had such brazen contact with human feces.

Basement Joe

The hostel was an original brownstone building constructed in the early part of the twentieth century. The stairs leading down to the basement had been replaced multiple times since then, yet they still creaked in spots because of the traffic upon them. The basement was the heartbeat of this hostel and the central gathering point for all comers.

Enjoying a day off by sleeping till the early afternoon, I descended the creaky hostel staircase intending to engage the basement denizens. The entryway at the bottom of the wooden staircase was open, the buzz of the television and of young foreign accents heard before hitting the last step. I was greeted by a welcoming committee in the seven or so couches and cushion seats. Their disrepair spoke of wanderers over more years than my life had known. A television under the street side window and a conspicuously placed pay phone were the room's primary ornaments.

In a room spattered with young travelers, some sprawled out napping on the couches, others sharing a cigarette and discussing their homelands or the sights of New York City or the plethora of things they hated about Americans, an older man sat on the edge of a deep blue couch abutting the side wall. He was black skinned with dark, wooly matted hair that receded above his brow. He was wrapped in a deep conversation with two young Americans.

I sat away from them at first, pretending to watch television, but listening to every word of their conversation. I worried I'd disrupt their good time, or worse their deep conversation. This might lead to them ignoring me or some other form of rejection. Neither of which were acceptable alternatives to sitting quietly and waiting for an invitation, or an appropriate opportunity to engage.

"Don't be surprised that life after death would come through a man," the older man said. "You know what the bible says, as one man brought sin into the world, well, another brings it out. So that's the way it is, you know."

These were the first words I heard from his mouth. I was taken aback. I had not formed a conscious impression of him, but whatever I thought of him in my subconscious was contrary to the words I heard him speak now.

"I'm just sayin', he's a man," replied the young traveler in a northeast accent. "It doesn't make sense that he could be God. How is a man going to keep me living forever?"

The older man looked at him pensively, allowing him to speak his mind.

"No way, no way I'm telling you," the young traveler continued. "Man made that shit up, that's all there is to it."

These were the words I expected to hear. I have found most travelers to be quite secular people. My intrigue, therefore, lay with the older gentleman. I listened as the conversation moved. The older man kept on with his preaching, inoffensive as a child, but with a discernable confidence lacking in the young traveler.

When the conversation waned, fatigued from such heavy topics, the young travelers split, one heading upstairs, the other going to watch television. The older man remained, sitting there on his blue couch as though on a throne; the lounge his kingdom. I found the courage to strike up my own words with him. He introduced himself as Joe.

"What brings you here?" I asked. "I don't guess I'm catching you on a tour of the east coast?"

"Oh, no," he replied, "I work here in the hostel and they give me a room down here."

"What's down here mean?" I asked. "There's nothing but a t.v. lounge and kitchen."

He pointed to a curtain in the corner behind the kitchen area, "Behind there, that's my room. Has been for 25 years." I looked to the corner, which had gone unnoticed until now. If anything, I thought it was a storage closet.

"But, Joe, how do you sleep?" I asked. "There are people down here all night, and the TV stays on too."

"Oh, I don't sleep at night." He replied. "I sleep during the day, in the morning."

"So what do you do all night?" I asked.

"Usually just watch C-Span." He replied.

"All night?" I asked.

"Not all night," he answered. "Til' about four in the morning."

"Do you read or anything?" I inquired.

"Yeah, well, sometimes." He said. "It is hard to read with all these people around."

I could not stop questioning silently, *How can you live in a room in a kitchen? How can you watch C-Span all night?* I thought it strange to watch Senate proceedings in the daytime, let alone through the night. Surprisingly, there wasn't much more to Joe's daily routine.

Joe actually reminded me of my grandfather in his chair at home. His left leg had been amputated as an old man, so he rarely got up from his olive green lazy-boy. All day long he sat, watching golf or reading large print Louis L'Amour novels. Joe was like that, but on account of his two legs and apparently healthy body, I couldn't explain his desire to live such a sedentary routine. Nor could I pull out much more from his life, other than growing up in Manhattan, even after thorough questioning. For all his strong opinions and love of conversation, I found him impossible to discover. He was an enigma I would love to unravel.

Mrs. Cohen's Whoop

Confidence is a foreign word to a medical student. It is akin to strange phrases like *raison d'être*. I knew what it meant generally, but it was far from my own vernacular. Most of medical school was spent gaining an intimate knowledge of this word. As I understood it, confidence was being comfortable with being uncomfortable. Not letting the patient sense your jittering stomach as you stick a needle through their skin or ask to examine their body where few people ever see. This takes confidence, and confidence is gained from experience. Experience occurs after making mistakes for a thousand days in a row. Such is the molding process of becoming a physician.

I took a leap towards confidence during my last night shift in the St. Luke's ER. An elderly Jewish woman named Mrs. Cohen came in complaining of a common ailment for people of her age: constipation. You really don't appreciate the importance of your plumbing until it goes to hell on you. She came into the ER ten days after her last bowel movement.

For all of medicine's advances, a finger in the rectum, recklessly breaking through clogged up stool, is still the treatment of choice for impacted bowels. Manual disimpaction is the medical term for the procedure. It is a word disdained by medical personnel the world over. Tonight I was going to gain some confidence in the lovely world of the rectal vault.

"No, I'm sorry. No, no, I don't want a medical student doing that." Replied Mrs. Cohen after my attending, Dr. Blackman, requested to let me gain confidence vis-à-vis her rectal vault. I had established great rapport with this patient, key for any disimpaction. I was a bit surprised when she disagreed to my performing the procedure.

"Right, I know ma'am. But you know we teach medical students here, right? This is a teaching hospital, right, so it is really important for our students, right, to learn how to do these procedures, right." Dr. Blackman used 'right' as his filler word. His speech was a constant stream of rights and chuckles which induced his phlegm-laden smoker's cough. It was annoying, but he was a nice attending who stuck up for my right to learn the medical trade.

He was persistent, and Mrs. Cohen was in too much pain to waste another minute with a colon full of dried feces. She finally acquiesced. The problem was that, in the process of convincing her, I had chimed in things like, "It's really okay, ma'am. I've done this plenty of times before." This was true. I had done plenty of digital rectal exams before. They say the only indication not to do a rectal on a patient with an abdominal complaint is if you don't have a finger or the patient doesn't have a rectum. The reality is that most medical students learn to do this exam on patients under general anesthesia. The difficulty, however, was not the procedure, but in asking for permission, "For the sole purpose of learning the practice of medicine, can I invasively exam the most sensitive part of your body?" There are few barriers to patient care more difficult to overcome from the perspective of the newly initiated medical student.

In any case, I had never done this procedure exactly. But by having to argue my case, I implied an element of mastery over this particular procedure. I implied confidence! An old friend of mine had the life motto, *Fake it til' you make it.* That simple catch phrase defines the process of learning clinical medicine. The medical student exudes a confidence not yet earned, and comforts a patient with knowledge he or she still lacks. And most distressing of all, the student performs invasive procedures with experience not yet gained. Tonight I was going to fake it and, pray God, I was going to make it.

Dr. Blackman walked me through the procedure, "Right, so you wanna lay the patient on their side, knees to their chest like you do for a rectal exam." He donned a latex rubber glove and doused his right index finger with Surgilube lubricant. He continued his teaching, "Enter the rectum and dig!"

All I could see was his hand. His index finger was off in the dry, caked plains of this poor lady's rectum. Dig he did, I tell you. The poor old lady was in obvious pain, but she endured. When he pulled his hand out there was a little pellet on his finger. For all that digging I expected more. I scarcely understood how he had not opened up a floodgate of feces.

"Right, there you go, Brian. That's it. Now you try. See one, do one, teach one." That is the official motto of medical education, a distant relative to *fake it till you make it.* Both mottos had me at a point where I was sending my unlearned finger off into no-man's land.

I gloved up, lubed up, apologized for any inconvenience and pain and re-iterated, "Don't worry about it, ma'am, I've done similar procedures before, plenty of times." With those parting words I sent my finger off in search of some deeply impacted confidence.

I went in, felt the dried feces and began scraping it with my finger. I pulled out another pellet and was overcome with joy. Dr. Blackman applauded my effort, "There you go Brian. Good. Get all you can, right, and come find me when you're done."

I felt some relief now. My attending and the patient had gained confidence in my ability to handle this job. I cleaned off my finger and went in for the next disimpaction. The next moment, however, my concentration was shattered by a loud, crackling whoop!

What followed were words that still ring in my mind's ear, and turn my face red in shame. From the head of the bed I heard an angry voice yell, "What in God's name, boy? You're in my vagina!"

I was mortified! I was worse than mortified. I froze out of sheer hope that I was dreaming, but quickly recognized the word "vagina" that continued to erupt from this woman's mouth.

"Oh my, I am so sorry, ma'am." These words came out of my mouth, but the rest of my being was searching for a dark hole to crawl into. Sadly, the ER was short on these 'medical student bunkers'. I had nothing to do but stand there and take the verbal beating I so rightly deserved.

"I knew it, I just knew it." Mrs. Cohen exclaimed. "I told you I didn't want a student doing this to me. Are you going to clean that up?"

It would've been forgivable if I'd landed in her vagina to start. But I had already pulled a pellet of poop from her rectum. My finger was covered in brown smears of E. coli when I lodged it into her vagina.

"I said, are you gonna clean that up?" She asked. She could not see my face. She only knew that there was a motionless and speechless medical student standing over her curled up backside.

I gathered myself and tried my best to pull off that ever difficult combo of confidence and caring. But now, my confidence level was shot to Hades and beyond. I wondered if I would ever find it again.

"Just a moment Mrs. Cohen, I will clean you off. I'm so sorry, I just…" My words tapered because they were meaningless. The act was complete. No words could change that. I went and got Dr. Blackman and some paper towels. He came back with me and reassured the patient that my hands would never touch her again. He would finish the disimpaction. I would be in the corner of an empty room sucking my thumb and dreaming of a waterfall.

After Dr. Blackman finished, I apologized for letting him down. In keeping with his good nature, he did not even poke fun at me.

"You won't make that mistake again, so don't worry about it." He said. "She'll be alright."

Aside from the discomfort on her part and the embarrassment on mine, I was also worried I may have deposited a vaginal infection into this woman. Dr. Blackman quickly sped off to another patient. I found a second year resident to help alleviate my anxiety.

Dr. Rogan was a spunky female with a raspy voice. She taught me something new about the vagina. With a hurried swatting motion of her hand she told me, "Don't worry about it. The vagina is a dirty place." She said it with all seriousness and sped off as well. So, the vagina is a dirty place. I don't remember what I thought of vaginal flora before, but I never thought it rivaled the large bowel.

Twenty minutes later, I mustered up the courage to speak with Mrs. Cohen. I wanted to apologize again and salvage any rapport with her that I had worked so diligently to burn away.

"How are you doing Mrs. Cohen?" I asked. "I wanted to apologize again for my mistake. I am so sorry. I really was being careful, I just…I guess I've still got a ways to go."

"Oh, don't worry about it." she replied. "I don't like medical students working on me 'cause it's hard on them and it's hard on me. But you don't worry about anything. I feel so good now!" I could scarcely believe her attitude towards me.

"I went for the first time in ten days." She said. "I feel so much better!"

If Mrs. Cohen could be happy to see me after I mistook her vagina for her rectum, then her relief knew no limits. She was all but glowing. Relief for the constipated is unparalleled in its power.

The greater lesson from my interaction with Mrs. Cohen was having the confidence to apologize for a mistake. Transparent honesty is the essence of bedside manner which, she taught me, is equally important as medical knowledge or mastery of procedural technique. I knew I would have a career full of mistakes to accompany this one, but with some insight I had seized a small victory in an otherwise monumental defeat.

Ties That Bind

The end of July came abruptly for me. The ER was exciting, though 10 hour shifts often dragged, with little time to reflect or think. Deep down, however, I was aware and very content to be living both ends of a dream. I was using medicine, which gave me stability, to gain understanding about myself and the world at large, a process of revelation that was inherently unstable. I had to give up comfort to find these pearls, shedding the familiar to gain perspective on my life. I was thankful for the opportunity.

Nevertheless, hostel life, while anonymous and liberating, drained my emotional state. I needed privacy and stability. I needed my wife. I had only one week at home with Shelley before returning to Manhattan for my next rotation.

New York City

I.M.

Boston on the Chinatown Bus

My fondest childhood memory is laying in the back seat of my parent's car as we drove down the interstate at night on family road trips. My headphones always played the same cassette tape: Boston, the first album. The passing darkness was broken only by stars and intermittent street lights, my mind opened up to all the dreams and visions of my heart. Anything was possible. I thought even then as a boy that if I could choose how I wanted to die, it would be driving off into the unknown just like that, under a full moon and stars, with Boston playing on my headphones.

As I headed back to New York City after my weeklong respite, the car was replaced by a $10 fare on the Chinatown bus line. These buses were famous on the poor student underground as the principle mode of transport from Boston to Manhattan. The music playing through my headphones was (usually) different, but the feeling was the same. The unknown future and the endless possibilities past every jog in the road drew my eyes to the window and would not let go. I didn't need to read or talk. Watching each town with its rows of houses, each city populated by brick and metal was enough to pass the time.

It is my road trip habit to throw two books into my navy blue JanSport backpack. The constant is a travel size Bible. It is for spiritual protection as much as for reading. The other is a novel. At various points in my fourth year I carried *Notes from the Underground,* by Fyodor Dostoevsky, *The Bell Jar,* by Sylvia Plath, *West with the Night,* by Beryl Markham, *The Heart of Darkness,* by Joseph Conrad, *Catcher in the Rye,* by

J.D. Salinger, and *Orthodoxy*, by G.K. Chesterton. The latter was not a novel, but a consuming read nonetheless.

For this leg of my journey, I carried *The Moviegoer*, by Walker Percy. Percy was an existentialist philosopher from the Deep South, a rare combination. He was a physician by training and never considered philosophy until he contracted Tuberculosis and found himself quarantined in a mountain top sanitarium. At minimal cost to his life and limb, he was removed from the rigors of his career and allowed to read, write, and think with his full attention. He never came back to medicine.

Between reading *The Moviegoer* and looking outside to stave off motion sickness, I was entertained by a young woman in front of me who had a large wooden birdcage in the center aisle. By the time we passed New Haven, Connecticut the bird was out on the woman's shoulder. The bus driver and attendant didn't even look up.

A half hour from our destination the bird pooped all over the woman's shoulder. She was preoccupied on her cell phone and didn't notice. I reached to notify her of the damage, but I paused when I heard her say, *"We're* so excited to get there!"

Projecting such human emotions on this bird confounded me. I withdrew my hand thinking that she actually might want the excrement there. It was evidence that the bird really couldn't wait to arrive.

The Chinatown stop in Manhattan was adjacent to the subway. I wasted no time hopping on the trains headed to the Upper Westside.

Maria's Four Walls

I found a new residence for my Advanced Internship in Internal Medicine at St. Luke's. I needed to put my clothes in a drawer and sleep behind four walls at night. I also wanted Shelley to visit me, something possible but impractical while staying in the hostel.

I found a room in the apartment of a spry elderly woman named Maria. The apartment was a seven minute walk from St. Luke's. The neighborhoods surrounding St. Luke's were very poor and filled with African Americans and Hispanics. Around the apartment was a dominant presence of immigrants from the Dominican Republic. Maria was counted among them.

Though impoverished and empty of opportunity, the neighborhoods were vivacious and full of life. To be sure, there were poorer places in New York City, but the discrepancy between the neighborhoods around 115th street and those around my hostel on 88th street could not have been greater. As a medical student, I was thankful for this population because the poor and the immigrants made for infinitely more interesting patients.

Maria had resided in the same apartment at 108th street for 30 years. In that time, she learned no more than ten words in English. She was no anomaly though. Spanish was spoken at every corner and in every shop. I often skipped the formality of English and presumed Spanish was the language of choice when ordering food or dropping clothes off at the laundromat.

The apartment's front door opened into a kitchen the size of a walk in closet. It served as a living and dining room as well. To the left was a small bathroom. To the right was a narrow hallway with two doors. One opened into Maria's room, the other to my room. The apartment walls were filled with gold foil images of Mary and Saints, along with second-hand religious calendars and scripture reminders. Only a plastic rooster above the refrigerator broke up the impoverished Catholic ambience.

Maria charged me $500 for the month of September. I was exceedingly fortunate to have found such cheap housing in the city. But Maria rented to me illegally. Her apartment was a holdover from the days of rent control in Manhattan. Her rent reflected a price from the 1970's. She was charging me more than her entire month's rent.

She requested I deny my residence in her apartment should the nosy super inquire what I was doing in the building. I didn't mind. I figured she deserved to make some extra cash in life. She told me she was saving money for a trip home to the Dominican Republic as she had not been home in over a decade.

My room had four white walls and a sense of privacy that made me very happy. Random pieces of furniture lined those walls without rhyme or reason. There were four armoires of different shades of wood, a television, and a small dorm room refrigerator. The centerpiece was a queen size bed with no comforter, just two white sheets. It had the elastic properties of a wrestling mat.

A green towel was laid caringly across the refrigerator. Maria provided this so I could take a shower. When I pulled the towel up it was pockmarked by wood chips and tiny hair locks. Twenty years had no doubt passed since its last use, although nothing explained the origin of the woodchips. Needless to say, a trip to the downtown Manhattan K-Mart was made on day number two. Like Mrs. Cohen, whose relief covered a multitude of transgressions, I took comfort in that room despite its faults.

Internal Medicine Advanced Internship

Advanced Internships are a month where the medical student morphs into a virtual intern. The student is to experience an increase in responsibility over their patients. Duties include placing orders, checking labs, and knowing everything there is to know about the patient and their disease, all this before presenting them on morning rounds to the attending physician each day.

I was nervous about this elective. I wanted more responsibility over patients, but medical knowledge was a continual battle for me. I never felt like I knew enough, or sometimes anything at all. What if I dropped the ball? What if I hurt a patient?

The reality is that increased responsibility for a medical student in the United States doesn't mean that much. CYA kept my signature meaningless and far away from drug ordering pathways. I was glad to wear the medical student's protective cloak, but a desire to break out was emerging. I wondered at times how long I would have to wait to step out on a limb and really learn medicine.

St. Luke's Medicine Team

St. Luke's Internal Medicine department has a number of different teams. A team consists of an attending, a third year resident, and two interns. There is a rotating system where the attending changes every two weeks, the resident and interns every four. My first attending, Dr. Greely, was a slow and methodical physician who spoke every sentence in a "lets talk this out and express ourselves completely" fashion. He took the same approach with his patients, who always appreciated his thorough approach and abundant communication.

The third year resident on my team, Brady Charleston, was the definition of cool. I first saw him as I walked into the resident work room on our floor. His hair was pulled back tight into a ponytail that landed at the back of his neck. He was without a white coat, with an off-white button down shirt and faded blue Dockers. The lack of a white coat is a sign of seniority in medicine. Medical students wear short white coats, interns and residents wear long white coats. Upper level residents like Brady, as well as fellows and attendings, follow their own preferences. Full professors then return to white coat wearing, only without the trappings of a junior physician such as review books and note cards. It is a strange longitudinal hierarchy.

Brady was somewhat informal, with shirt sleeves rolled to just below the elbow, and no tie. He had a thin, muscular frame evidenced by pectoral muscles that converged at the top of his sternum. He carried an aura, and the tan, of a beach bum who had been in the city too long.

In the world of medicine, assimilation is the rule, and even though Brady hinted at rebellion with his dress and physical presence, his demeanor was that of a solid physician. He was quick to appreciate a joke or a funny story, but was otherwise business minded, and he had to be. His job was to monitor all of the patients under the teams' care and to make sure the interns were doing their jobs. This was no small task considering an intern was only weeks removed from medical school. Their learning curve was steep and painful.

The two interns on my team were a girl named Dubersky and an Argentinean guy named Viola. I think that the preface "Doctor" was the only way to justify a name like Dubersky. She was someone who should have been in research, but found herself stuck in a profession that required tremendous people skills. Dubersky never joked with a patient, or even a colleague. I did see her smile at a lunchtime Cardiology lecture the second week of my rotation, but she was clearly out of her element. Perhaps she never examined herself enough to consider another path in life, like one leading to a bench and a microscope.

Viola was a bit different. Though his people skills were not standard setting, I sensed he enjoyed interacting with patients. He was from Argentina and had aced the U.S. Medical Licensing Exams (USMLE). If not for the relaxed mentality inherited from South American culture, he would have been wound pretty tight. He treated me respectfully and with interest from the first time we met, which I considered a significant victory from my lowly medical student position.

Axolotl

I found a seat in the back of the small room next to Brady, who pulled a seat over for me. That small act of kindness broke my initial perception that he was too cool to interact with a medical student. I tried not to be rigid making quick judgments on people, but I also trusted my instincts. Fortunately, my gut instinct this time was totally wrong.

Greely, our methodical attending, was leading a discussion about one of the sicker patients on the service. Brady was recounting a procedure he had done on this patient when Greely's cell phone went off. He listened intently and without interrupting the person on the other end, looked up at Brady and mouthed the word "Code".

A code is when the medical staff performs life saving resuscitation on a patient. Dubersky and Brady bolted out the door. I froze in place having no idea where my place was yet on this team. Greely looked at me as he flipped his cell phone closed, surprised I was still seated.

"Well," he asked, "are you going to go?"

I jumped up immediately and sped off down the hall.

I was last to arrive at the code. There was a mass of people in the room and an energy I had never felt before. Not even in the Emergency Room. There was pressure in the air and it pressed upon me like a wet blanket. I counted 13 people in the room, not including the man lying on the bed getting his chest pounded on every second.

This hodge-podge group of doctors and nurses worked like a fine-tuned machine. In spite of the apparent chaos, there was no doubling up of work. This was due to the man standing behind the defibrillator, out of everybody's way. He was the "eye-in-the-sky."

"I want the defibrillator on his chest now." He called out. "What are his most current vital signs?"

As a pheromone calls forth the worker ants to their task, everything happened at his order. The shock pads were placed, one on top of the chest, the other over his left side. A nurse standing nearby sternly reported his blood pressure and pulse. The "eye-in-the-sky" took everything in, quietly calculating what the next step should be in a well defined life saving protocol.

"You're all doing great. Keep it up." He said. "All in a day's work!"

His attitude brought calm to everyone in the room as they faced death literally in the face. I stood back in awe of his demeanor and knowledge and wondered how long it took to gain that tacit confidence. More importantly, how was I supposed to get to that point? Would my journey to that spot be lined by tombstones I helped create?

These thoughts are not unique. Medical students always think of knowledge under the dimension of time. Our lives are filled with enormous pressure to know tomes of information. The thought of a finite end to this harsh reality consumes us. Watching that attending, fully confident that right answers were only a neuronal buzz away filled me with hope that I could arrive there, some day.

I crashed down from these contemplative clouds when Dubersky pushed me aside on her way to the bedside. I finally saw the patient between all the people and the machinery hovering over him.

I saw a thin, naked black man of fifty or sixty years. He held a still look in his eyes. I did not break my gaze away from his body. How could I? He was caught in a place from where nobody returns, but he was not yet gone. The crowd scurried around the man, reaching for needles, medicine, gauze, and tubes. Over a five minute eternity, it became apparent his body was not responding to the resuscitation protocol. Finally, the "eye-in-the-sky" called the code and the patient was pronounced dead.

Bodies fell away from my field of vision as my eyes fixated on his quiet body. The chaos that had given the room a sensation of pressure, dropped back like an ocean tide. I was soon alone with this man, and not even a man, just a body. His lifeless form lay there, eerily still, his eyes closed by a gracious hand of the living.

Where was he now? Where was that being that existed on this earth, loved a woman, seeded children, and cared for others? Were we nothing more than cells and tissue and salt? I was utterly consumed by the lack of life in that body. A life which, only hours ago, was asking the nurse for a cup of water or smiling at a visitor to his bedside. In a year's time, that man's existence would be nothing more than a memory of a few other mortal souls whose time would also surely come, just not today.

I felt no kinship to this body, no remorse and no grief. It was only metaphysical selfishness that consumed me, manifested as sadness for the gravity of the family's situation, and how they would yelp and mourn for this loss of life. In that sense, and in that moment, the tide rolled in again. With the heaviness came the realization that all the struggling and fighting was not for this poor soul. No, it was only to prevent the conversation now taking place with the family. Life postmortem was the concern of the patient; a crushed spirit was the concern of the physician.

The fog of war is the part of a conflict that separates the plan on paper, and the actual reality on a battlefield. It is the smoke and haze caused by opposing forces, unforeseen strengths and weaknesses, and the ability and will of the man on the ground. Reading life support protocols was innocent and academic, while here the battle plan was riddled with guilt. Where was the power to save? What did all that scientific knowledge mean to this patient now? The truth is, there is a fog in medicine too, and I was standing in the middle of it.

When I finally walked out of the room, the body was completely alone. It was as naked as the day he came into this world, not even a blanket covered it. I remembered a story called *Axolotl* by the Argentinean Julio Cortázar. A young boy visits an aquarium every day to stare into the *ojos de oro* (golden eyes) of the aquatic salamander known as the Axolotl. So transfixed is he by this fish, he becomes trapped in the body of the fish. He now views the world from inside the tank looking out. I was similarly trapped in the body that lay before me, stranded on a high wire connecting life and death. I was clamoring for one, but inexorably creeping towards the other.

This was my first experience with death as a medical student. I knew that very day that a memory was just etched into a deep recess of my mind, even my soul. I would never forget the controlled chaos of the code, the perspiration of young doctors proving their metal, the cold stares of doctors with nothing more to prove, and the stillness of a dead body punctuating the vain efforts of each. I took solace that it was not my hands pounding his chest or squeezing oxygen into his lungs. It was not my eyes that would burn holding back tears facing his wife. Death would touch my hands eventually. It was the nature of my profession. But thankfully, it would not touch them today.

Red Beans and City Lights

Shelley's first visit came at a good time. I had a golden weekend which meant my team was not on call. I did not have to set foot in that hospital Saturday or Sunday. I wanted to explore New York City with my wife, and watch the eyes of someone who has never craned their neck at a Manhattan skyline or been overwhelmed by the elbows and knees of a crowded subway.

Shelley arrived on the Greyhound bus from Boston on Saturday in the early afternoon. Not unexpectedly, I got there just a few minutes late and found her sitting in front of a newsstand in the middle of Penn Station. Her blonde hair touched down to her shoulders and a pair of cheap sunglasses acted like a headband holding her bangs off her forehead. She was pale skinned even in the middle of summer, but the milky white texture only brought out the blue of her eyes and she never strikes me as less than beautiful.

She had her green and black backpack sitting at her feet. It's her favorite piece of luggage because it opens like a suitcase, but wears like a backpack. She is always happy when she gets to use that backpack, and by the look on her face I could tell it was so. She looked intensely fixated, on nothing in particular, yet everything around her at the same time.

Hordes of people came and went. Shelley watched them all meticulously. A woman sauntered by in a white tank top that left bare her lower belly and back which was covered in green and red tattoos. Her arm had Chinese script written down from joint to joint. Shelley's eyes locked onto this woman and didn't release until she was swallowed by the mass of people shuffling through the station. I was going to hear about that one very soon, no doubt. Shelley is a people watcher extraordinaire, and this quality almost singlehandedly made me fall in love with her. At least it told me this was someone I could pass the hours with, maybe even the years.

I waited myself, people watching as she was, except that I was fixated on her. She wore blue jeans and a pair of Reef sandals, and a green shirt with a modest plunge in the neckline. She did this for me I knew, because she is very modest about her chest, which draws stares no matter what she wears. After our time apart she was trying to impress me, and it was working.

I appreciated the simple opportunity to watch her without her noticing. The more intertwined two lives become, the less opportunity one has to voyeuristically view the other. At the movies or out to dinner with friends, we sit next to each other. Walking through a park, we hold hands and walk side by side. Much like our own selves, we never see the other from a distance. I don't watch her gait or the way her body moves in three dimensions. I don't notice the way her eyes track a passerby. I do notice these things in the rest of the world. It is a cruel paradox of close relationships.

Now I longed for her as time away will cause a man to do. A surge of desire rushed through me to be reunited with this woman. It was a curious feeling, and not purely sexual. There was an emotional attachment incomprehensible to me before meeting and spending five years with Shelley. Now it was acutely noticeable as we spent more and more of this fourth year apart.

When I walked myself into her line of vision, an excited grin swept across her face. She stood up tall and walked with purpose towards me. Her legs were long and athletic, obvious even through her blue jeans, gliding with her peculiar gate that is as defining as the ocean blue iris of her eyes. She bobs forward, subtly, with each step landing in a lean on the back on her heels, a genetic trait inherited directly from her father. She approached me, lunging the final inches, giving momentum to her kiss. Her lips were soft and wet, engaging my own lips until her face slipped onto my shoulder. I held her until she knew I was still hers.

We left Penn Station and took a city bus uptown. We arrived back to the apartment just a few minutes before Maria, who came in the house wearing a humongous sun hat whose brim kept her shoulders in shadows. I introduced her to Shelley, translating their conversation.

She was clearly enamored by Shelley. I knew this not by her insistence in giving Shelley her silver Chinese slippers to wear around the house. It was the wide smile she cracked for her. Maria was very congenial, but her face was not a pleasant one. It was bronzed with age and her mouth labored not to frown, like gravity and pain had pulled her skin toward the ground. For Shelley, however, it became bright and open, defying the forces pulling against it.

"Would you like some food? I can make you some eggs." She offered. Eggs were the only food item in her refrigerator. Apart from a small yellow carton of Arm & Hammer Baking Soda, the refrigerator was perpetually empty. I wasn't sure what Maria ate to survive, besides those eggs.

Shelley scanned the kitchen. Next to the stove was an open window leading out to the courtyard of the apartment complex. On the window sill was a cluster of bananas that sat next to a thin layer of bird feces. Pigeons often perched on that sill and left their markings.

If that were overlooked there were still the rat traps checkering the floor in visible crevices by the refrigerator and stove. The floor was a fake brown tile that curled up at the baseboards, giving endless cover to rodents of all sizes. Shelley flashed me a subtle glance that screamed, "We are not eating here!"

"No thank you, Maria." I said to her in Spanish. "We're going to eat out tonight." We finished cleaning up, got dressed and left for Times Square.

There is nothing that exists on earth that can't be found in New York City. Every nationality, every food, every fetish can be quenched in the Big Apple. And you needn't stray far from Times Square to do it.

The path from the subway car to the street was labyrinthine at the Times Square stop. Shelley and I followed signs as best we could and still found ourselves backtracking. At every turn there were homeless performers doing sometimes amazing acts for cash and coin tossed into hats or guitar cases.

We saw more than one group of black teenage youths performing Capoeira, the acrobatic Brazilian fight-dance performed in pairs to music, as you would imagine it in Rio de Janeiro. Their faces gleamed with bright smiles, their bodies raw with muscle and youth. They performed in the dungeons of the subway as if they owned the world.

Walking up the final staircase we exited the subway maze and entered Times Square. Entry into that glamorous urban circus causes sensory overload. It is like the transition to flight when skydiving. The senses are overpowered by the size, speed, and persistence of the stimulus. It doesn't even pulsate, it doesn't allow for a breath. We stopped in our tracks and stared.

It hardly seemed the sun had set. Advertisements glittered and flashed. The NASDAQ broadcast its stream of numbers across digital banners. Television news shows played on giant screens. Mega stores for Virgin Records, Hershey's, and Toys-R-Us were stacked in improbable accord across the urban horizon.

Sean 'P. Diddy' Combs loomed 1,000 times larger than life from a photo image on the side of a skyscraper. ABC, MTV,

Disney, every major media outlet was represented in that square mile. Even the military had its Armed Forces Recruiting Station on a traffic island between Broadway and 7th Ave., right in the middle of the action.

Shelley and I walked with our necks craned towards the skyline. We had no choice in the matter. We were reduced to zombies feeding off of the marketing glitz that pierced us to our capitalist core. We were reawakened twice by cars zooming by within inches of our kneecaps. We didn't notice when our feet walked the sidewalks or the streets, our eyes could not bother with the ordinary texture of concrete and asphalt.

As we acclimated to the environs we did come down to eye level. The people in this urban jungle were legion. Most were slick looking, dressed in dark black clothing. Some wore formal attire, heading to a Broadway show on any of the side streets around Times Square. Some headed to restaurants or clubs, which were found behind every flashing bulb.

The rest were either poor folks or tourists, both of whom wandered without a particular destination. That included Shelley and me, on both accounts. We walked up and down the main drag and every side street. As we walked under the glow of theater billboards lining 47th Street, I heard a voice call out behind me, "Brian?"

I turned back and my eyes fell on Mary Tetzlaff, a face I never thought I'd see again. She was my Zoology lab partner freshman year at LSU. It was my first collegiate science course and I was hopelessly confounded by the details of bench science. Swabbing agar plates, flaming wire loops over Bunsen burners, dissecting frogs, I was lost in the minutia of recipe science.

Mary took me for a dumb jock and balked at my proposal to join up as lab partners. I was persuasive though and she took me on condition that even if I was a dumb jock, I was not permitted to act like one. In the end, we proved a solid team and decent friends. We spoke in other shared classes but I didn't see her much afterwards. Last I heard she was headed to LSU medical school in New Orleans.

We spoke for only a few minutes on that curbside. She stood with two other girlfriends, classmates of hers at LSU medical school. They were heading inside the theater for a show. I told her I was finishing up medical school as well. She did not act surprised in the least, which reminded me of something I always liked about Mary. She always believed in me. She trusted I would work hard in the lab, and she always told me I would get into medical school.

I walked away from our encounter in Times Square with a surprising sense of encouragement. So often I felt incompetent or fumbling through tasks I was ill-suited to accomplish. Seeing Mary reminded me how long I had been fumbling. Whether I was growing E. coli in a Petri dish or answering the attending's request for the 19 causes of digital clubbing, I never felt adequate. I needed to remember that I was not lost on this long road of medicine. I would get through it like I got through everything else, with perseverance.

There was no question about where to eat that evening when we saw a familiar storefront awning among the thousands of restaurants in Times Square. The jumbled red letters of Popeye's Chicken & Biscuits shone like a beacon to our Louisiana eyes. I usually scoff at the idea of fast food, especially in a place like New York City. But I know something that people outside of Louisiana are not privy too: Nobody does Red Beans & Rice better than Popeye's. If you are a Louisiana restaurant south of Interstate-10, whether hole-in-the-wall or upscale, you had better be good if you are going to survive. You have to prepare well the staples of the Cajun diet: Jambalaya, Po'Boy sandwiches, Gumbo, Boiled Crawfish, and the most ubiquitous dish of all, Red Beans & Rice. Popeye's was made famous by New Orleans native Al Copeland. I grew up walking by his New Orleans home at Christmas time to see the lights he put up.

Nobody matched Copeland's for Christmas extravagance. And nobody had a Lamborghini in their driveway you could walk up to. His was red. It is the only Lamborghini I have ever touched. Copeland has other restaurants, including a high-end place that carries his namesake. They sell a Red Beans & Rice that costs $10 a bowl. The bit of secret knowledge I have is that his version at Popeye's fast food restaurant is one and the same. Same recipe, same taste, but it only costs $2.50. I never pass up a Popeye's for gourmet quality Red Beans & Rice, and I had not seen one for a whole year, since I last visited Louisiana.

Our night in Times Square turned into a reunion of old faces, tastes, and smells. It struck me as odd that in a place so crowded and so foreign, I would find so much familiar. I was deeply confused and drowned my bewilderment with a large cup of Popeye's Red Beans & Rice.

Ground Zero

The next morning Shelley packed up for the Greyhound back to Boston. We had only one errand to run before catching her 2:00 PM departure from the Port Authority Bus Terminal. It was time to visit a place neither of us had ever been, Ground Zero.

When we left the apartment, Maria was sitting at the kitchen table. This was the only piece of furniture outside of the bedrooms. This centerpiece was a two-person folding table, the same kind you would throw up hastily at a birthday party.

Maria sat there alone listening to the radio, staring through the transparent plastic table cover. The tablecloth was decorated with Christmas trees. The radio broadcast a morning program playing old Latin favorites. It sounded like Frank Sinatra in Spanish.

"She's so sad!" Shelley said to me after breaking into the Sunday morning air. "I get depressed watching her live that way."

"At least she's out of her bedroom." I replied. "For as long as I've been here she's been in her bedroom or the kitchen." She was not unlike Joe in that regard. She had a routine of social isolation that seemed to be self-inflicted. At least Joe had the hostel environment to live with, but Maria was utterly alone.

Shelley and I approached Ground Zero, in the heart of Manhattan's Financial District. When we reached the pedestrian area on Trinity Place, I was shocked by the nothingness that consumed the space of at least two square city blocks. The emptiness was not limited to the ground. It drifted up, cutting a hole in the atmosphere leading out of the city towards the sky. The presence of the buildings was still there, like a missing child whose place is still set at the family table.

The Ground Zero perimeter was surrounded by a chain link fence which we, and hundreds of other tourists, peered through. It was a workspace crawling with cranes, pavers, bulldozers, and workers. The level of the ground was still well below street level and offered no signs of climbing higher. The magnitude of what was before, and what was now, frightened me. To think that a group of individuals, part of no army or government, could wield that kind of power enraged me. The vulnerability the attacks exposed in my own psyche had yet to heal over.

I was always struck that my mother could tell me in such detail where she was when John F. Kennedy was shot. I wondered if I would ever have such a moment in my life; a transcendent memory I could share with any other American. And here it was before me, the scar from my generation's defining moment.

I had been in Israel when the events of September 11 took place. It had been strange to watch images of chaos and destruction beaming into Israel; they were usually beamed out of the Middle East to the United States. I was brought to tears by the vulnerability of being attacked without warning. All I had wanted that day was to be near my family, my people. Standing before that open grave of my countrymen at Ground Zero, the same closeness to America consumed me as it did years before. My opinions towards divisive political topics melted away and I united, by sorrow and fear, to my fellow citizen.

We walked the perimeter gauging every angle, letting the image sink into our deeper memories. This was not a place, or a moment, to ever forget. So we were surprised to find that noon was so quickly upon us. We left after a few half starts and turn backs to catch one more glimpse, finally agreeing that not missing Shelley's Greyhound bus was the only legitimate reason to break our eyes away.

Shelley and I stood together at the Penn Station gate waiting for the Boston bus to rev up. Our time together was short, and had gone by even faster. We wouldn't see each other again until I left New York in two weeks, at the end of my Internal Medicine rotation. That was the good news, actually, because I'd be leaving again shortly after that respite for Montana. One month I would be there, and there would be no weekend visits. Keeping our sights purposefully narrow, we talked only of getting through the next two weeks.

I watched her as she boarded that bus. It was another opportunity to see her move in three dimensions. Shelley never looked the same to me, not once from one day to the next. Today, her blonde hair came straight down and folded over her shoulders which were pulled erect by the weight of her backpack. She wore pink eye shadow but otherwise her lips were soft and a dulled red, and her cheeks were smooth and unaffected by the hot weather outside. I couldn't tell if she was even wearing makeup. Louisiana girls are deceptive like that, with tricks passed down through the generations that make you think they're not even trying.

I watched her through the bus windows wherever the blue curtains were pulled back. She made her way to a backseat, and looked at me. She smiled and I could see her white teeth, straight as only teenage braces can make them. She waved to me and her lips mouthed the words "I love you", though I knew she was really saying "Elephant Shoes" just to be funny. A surge of adrenaline rose within me, and I moved forward, but

my desire to close the distance was crushed by the wheels of the
bus pulling out of the station.

The Anderson Legacy

There were other medical students rotating through St.
Luke's Internal Medicine department. A few were students from
my program in Israel. A few others were Columbia University
medical students. I was thankful for one particular Columbia
student named Nicholas Anderson. This fellow achieved a task
I once thought impossible. He made me look sparkling in front
of the attending physician.

Nicholas Anderson was an example of legacy in medicine.
Legacy is the collective memory of the medical establishment
for those who had ever taken up the cloth. If your parents are
doctors, especially famous ones like Anderson's, you have
a linear shot at becoming one yourself. Sadly, little regard is
given to whether you should be a doctor at all.

The grand favor Anderson did for me was to arrive late
every chance he could. The first attending switch came at the
beginning of my second week on the ward. I knew things were
amiss when I showed up early Monday morning and saw Brady
Charleston with a tie on. Granted, it loosely fit around his neck,
with the collar not well folded around the backside. The necktie
button was unfastened and the two lengths of the tie sat apart
from each other as though in a dispute.

"What's up, bro?" I asked. "Why the formality? Are we
under surveillance or something?"

"New attending today. Dr. Young." He replied. "He runs a
tighter ship than Greely."

"Well, you wear it well." I said with a wide grin on my face.
He looked back at me knowingly.

Morning rounds started at 8:00 AM. Per Dr. Young's
request, we did walking rounds instead of the sit down rounds
we did with Greely. This meant we heard each presentation at

the doorway of the patient's room. By 8:40 AM we stood by the door of our second patient. My hips were aching already, and no slouching position in my extensive repertoire relieved the pain.

We were in the middle of a quick review from Dr. Young about the various causes of blood clots when the elevators opened up across from us and produced the smirking legacy-in-vivo that was Anderson. He sauntered up to the group and did not hide himself. There was no shame upon his countenance.

Surprisingly, Dr. Young did not stop his talking. I was embarrassed, wondering if Dr. Young was going to grill him. Instead, rounds went on. After three hours of standing in place, we finally finished. It was not until talking to Brady a week or two later that I found out what Dr. Young thought that morning. Brady told me Dr. Young asked him if he knew why Anderson was late. When Brady didn't know, he inquired, "What the hell is wrong with that guy then?" Apparently, Anderson never explained his tardiness to anyone.

Perhaps Dr. Young was not privy to the great opportunity he had in tutoring young Anderson. Why, his father had an entire medical hall named after him at a medical school in Pennsylvania. Legacy never has to explain its tardiness, only remind you of its right to be there.

Anderson's pattern of lateness made me look like a fiend for punctuality. I could not have been more thankful because I have never been purposefully early for anything in my life. There are times I have the hour mistaken and so arrive early. Generally, I am only comfortable when it takes a maddening combination of luck, chance, and good old fashioned hustle to get somewhere on time. That Anderson sacrificed his own punctuality for my benefit is something for which I remain grateful.

The LOTIL and Bush's Guns

Monday evening after work, I made a trip to the corner grocery store between Maria's apartment and Central Park. I picked up what I thought to be essential to my continued survival: cereal, milk, my own bananas, generic Macaroni & Cheese, and a small pan of ready-made cornbread. When I got home, I turned on the television Maria had set up in my room. I sat on the edge of my wrestling mat to eat dinner and fulfill a very high spot on the LOTIL.

The LOTIL is my running *List of Things I Love*. It is my firm belief that everyone should know what they love, and should keep some kind of track on it. It is an anchor in times of trouble, when it's hard to remember that anything is good. For example, eating any non-icing cake, like this cornbread, with a glass of cold milk is #3 on my LOTIL. This particular item is rooted in my Grandmother's kitchen in New Orleans, which I never entered as a kid without finding a chocolate chip bundt cake without icing sitting next to a tall glass of cold milk. And so it was in Maria's apartment, letting that doughy conglomeration of corn fall apart with a swig of cold 2% Milk was pure joy, as much for its taste as that it reminded me of home.

Some items on my LOTIL are things I've seen that always strike a chord in me. Waterfalls, for example, happen to be number one on my LOTIL. I will hike for days to find a waterfall, and I can stare at them for even longer. I like to find an individual drop at the top and follow it down, bouncing off of rocks until it reaches the pool below, where it is once again swallowed up into an indiscriminate mass. Other items are just whims, like train rides and building fires. They're simple things, but they always make me happy. The greatest joy of all is that my LOTIL items remain accessible throughout my life. That is why I keep track of them, so I can remember where to turn when my enthusiasm wanes.

The television was playing highlights of the presidential candidate debates between the much maligned Leader of the Free World, George W. Bush, and his contender in 2004, John Kerry. It was September and the election was heating up with only two months to go. The proxy War on Terror in Iraq was going strong with daily reports of U.S. and coalition casualties. Kerry was defending himself against a Swift Boat scandal and his decision to vote for the war, before voting against it. This would be a tight race.

Maria knocked on my half opened door to say hello. As the door swung open she glanced at the television. When she saw Bush's face on the screen, her eyes lit up. In Spanish she exclaimed, "Ay Dios Mio, this president of ours wants oil. And he is willing to kill our children for it!"

I was taken aback by her excitement. Till that point we had only discussed the importance of religion and prayer and the Virgin Mary, and I held my tongue whenever my Protestant ways disagreed. I did not respond to her initial statement, I only nodded and gave her a prodding, "Si?" She continued in her high-pitched, song-like voice, "I just don't understand, Ay Dios. This man is bad!"

Besides the wildness in her eyes, which burned like a fire right behind their sockets, Maria's tone troubled me. It reminded me of a lesson I had learned in my pre-marital counseling sessions with Shelley. Whenever you blew up over something, especially something small like passing the salt shaker the wrong way, you could bet that something else was going on. The root of the explosion was not what it seemed on the surface. A more fundamental issue was at play that had been ignored and unresolved, festering and building up pressure like a kettle with the lid closed. The explosion was inevitable.

With this in mind, I prodded Maria to keep talking about her feelings on the war. She continued, "Bush doesn't understand, he doesn't understand. My son was only 18 years old. He was killed by a gun. Bush thinks that he will solve everything with guns. He only kills our children, and for what? He doesn't understand."

"What happened, Maria?" I asked. "What happened to your son?"

She didn't answer me initially. The fire in her eyes was melting into a small pool of tears gathering over her lower eyelids, though none fell down her face. I sensed that I was treading a thin line, asking her about this very sensitive, and volatile, event in her life.

"He was just a boy, an innocent boy. But the streets are not innocent. Other boys fought but my son was shot. He didn't carry a gun. He didn't carry a gun."

I didn't understand all the words she used, she was falling back into some Dominican slang, which she had not done with me previously. Frankly, I didn't need to understand every word, her eyes said as much as her mouth. And what words did I possess in any language that would assuage her pain? The cold but empathetic stare is mastered by every medical student early in clinical medicine. I was grateful for the training I had in that regard. It didn't make this conversation easier, but it helped me give her the respectful ear she so obviously needed.

She looked back at the presidential debate. She didn't say anything about Bush, she just stared. For her, the topics of their conversation were secondary, like a distant moon orbiting around but never touching the only issue that mattered to her. And there was nothing to do about it anyways.

I bit my tongue from prodding her with further questions, much as that is against my nature. I sensed that the boy she described was a young man. As far as I knew, he had been her only son. I wanted so badly to dig deeper about the details of his death, to find out how she had dealt with such a traumatic blow. But couldn't I see quite clearly how this seminal event went on to define the rest of her life? She carried out a sad and lonely existence, living in a tomb of a bedroom which she left only for purposeful errands. It seemed to take all of her will to pass through a given day. She was isolated and unconnected to even her immediate surroundings in the apartment, on the block, in the city. She never spoke of friends, and she never went out to meet anyone for tea or coffee. Pain, it seems, had replaced hope.

This was the gravity that pulled so heavily upon her. Her soul was like rubble from a blast she alone had to swallow.

She left the room without saying another word. She went into her room and closed the door behind her. Further insight into her world did not come often during my month in her apartment. She spent most of every day right there in her bedroom. While only a thinly plastered wall separated our rooms, I never saw the inside of it. Only once did I even get a glimpse.

The Saturday after Shelley's visit I had a rent issue requiring Maria's attention. The kitchen was empty so I knocked on her bedroom door.

"*Esperate!*" I heard from within, along with some shuffling feet and the unlatching of three different locks. The door opened only slightly, enough for Maria to poke her head through. Behind her it was dark except for the blue light emanating from the television. I could make out only some iconic images on her wall, but their identity was obscure.

Maria's head was in front of me now, but the rest of her body was hidden in the room. She wore her same old moo-moo. I hardly noticed at first, but something about Maria's ears struck me as odd. Trying not to stare, I saw that herbal leaves were packed into both ear canals. The flowery ends were budding out and pointing in every direction. I wanted so badly to ask her what she was doing to herself. I held my tongue only because I didn't want her to feel discovered. Like Joe's sleep schedule, this was a quirk that only added to her mystique. I could only imagine what else had gone on over the last quarter century in that room she rarely vacated.

Pablo's legs

On the Internal Medicine ward patients ran me through a gauntlet of emotions. Of the legion I felt at one time or another, three were guaranteed: frustration, bewilderment, and utter sadness.

Pablo was the name we gave him. A short, stout illegal alien from Mexico with no documents, his original name was Arturo, and we called him by that name for the first two days he was on our service. Sometime during the second day he told us, adamantly, that his name was Jose. On his third morning it became Pablo. Realizing the pattern, we kept this one. Besides, we all thought he looked like a Pablo.

Pablo's connections to this country were frail, and his English language skills were non-existent. He came to the hospital with no family, no friends, nobody that could even vouch for his true identity or history. The other thing he showed up with was a belly that seemed to be impregnated with quadruplets. His belly button was everted from the pressure inside and his flanks were swollen wide. There was really only one disease that caused such a presentation: Liver cirrhosis. In a man Pablo's age, this was invariably due to alcoholism.

When alcohol kills off enough liver cells, the body becomes depleted of albumin, a protein that holds fluid in the blood vessels. When albumin drops, fluid leaks into the abdominal cavity, slowly filling it like water in a balloon. The other problem with not having a liver is that blood is not detoxified anymore. This leads to a change in mental status called encephalopathy.

It took the better part of a week to determine whether Pablo's problem was the language (though Viola and I and a few nurses all spoke to him in Spanish), the possible encephalopathy, or if he was just plain stupid. It was astonishing how many doctors were working to figure out the mystery behind Pablo's inability to understand the world around him.

Our frustration with Pablo was his legs. He used them constantly. He began walking the morning of the second day and the next time he laid down was the afternoon of the third day! He paced the floor for over 30 hours. For the most part he stayed local to his room and kept to himself. Sometimes he drifted into other rooms, talking or just staring at other patients.

All the while his belly protruded so far out that he could not button his hospital gown.

The look in his eyes was of someone in a very distant place. His words were coherent but their content illogical. He stopped me continuously in the halls insisting I let him out because, "all of my clothes are in that building over there." He pointed to the other wing of the hospital separated by a street and sidewalk.

When I tried reasoning with him, he only became fixated on my pager and reached for it. Tug-of-war matches with my hip as the fulcrum ensued. As pointless as it was to resist, his obtrusions were becoming increasingly difficult to ignore.

Pablo was, at times, as endearing as a little child. During one of our morning rounds we all stood in the hallway discussing a patient. Pablo walked by, shuffling along in his raggedy flip-flops. He passed us and then imperceptibly took a place behind Brady. He stood there, peering up at Brady with a smile you could drive a truck through.

Dr. Young stopped in the middle of his sentence and we all turned to stare at Pablo, including Brady. There was silence in the group. Pablo was fixated on Brady, smiling away and lost in his world, unable to break his gaze. It was a moment of grand comedic pause, broken by our inability to hold back our laughter. Even Dr. Young, generally a silent laugher, let out an audible chuckle. Brady escorted Pablo down the hall so we could continue rounds.

Moments of amusement aside, thirty hours of walking caused a great deal of frustration for hospital staff. His altered mental state meant that we had to guard him against exiting the floor, either through the elevator, stairs, or straightaway through the window. He was placed on 1:1 surveillance, having a nurse or security guard next to him at all times.

By the 30th hour, the staff was beyond their wit's end. Pablo was more and more active and beginning to disturb other patients. His refusal to get into his bed exacerbated matters. We began physically 'assisting' him in doing this. Escalation in his persistence and our frustration, especially Viola's, led to an executive decision to use medical weaponry against him. The weapon of choice was intramuscular diazepam. This drug knocked out a large man in minutes.

Giving it in the muscle was important. Pablo was not going to cooperate enough for us to put something in a vein, and he sure wasn't going to swallow something by mouth. With the help of a security guard, a nurse, and me, Viola stuck the needle into his upper left arm. There was a perceptible expiration by everyone on the floor when Pablo was finally put to bed.

Pablo slept for ten hours straight. When he awoke, he started walking again. Viola wasted little time in re-dosing him with diazepam.

It was hard to be mad at Pablo, as frustrating as he was for everyone. Maybe he was a fun and jovial guy when out drinking with his buddies. We were seeing a side that he was not born with, a side caused by a disease.

Pablo's disease was terminal by the time we saw him. He had six months or less to live, no matter what therapy we gave him. That made looking at him every day all the more frustrating. We spent a week trying to turf him to some other ward in the hospital, like psychiatry, or to another holding place. But when you are an illegal immigrant with a terminal illness, willing takers are hard to find. Ultimately, we convinced a Catholic organization to take custody of him. Bless their humble souls.

Subway Evangelist

My medical school's program office was located uptown at Columbia University Medical Center. I took off an afternoon from the Internal Medicine ward to tend to logistical business at that office. There was much to prepare since I would be going to Montana, Kenya, and then back to Israel for graduation in May.

I could have been upset at spending the afternoon signing paperwork, but to get there and back I had to ride the New York City subway. Vagrants, models, businessmen, laborers, tourists and immigrants hopped on and off those rails with religious consistency. It was a people watcher's paradise. A novelist hungry for inspiration would do well to buy a three day pass and ride continuously.

After my meetings, I took the C train down from 168th to meet a friend near St. Luke's, which was the 116th Street stop. I often used my subway time to study Bates' Guide to Physical Examination textbook. Today, it was hard to focus. It was late afternoon and the train was full of the usual suspects. Everyone had a seat except for a tall black man standing in front of the exit door in the middle of our subway car. He was not interested in sitting down.

He stood there with a beat up guitar strung with cheap nylon strings. He strummed simple chord progressions and sang worshipful songs. His body moved against the rhythm of the train to maintain his balance but his head was thrust back, his eyes gazing above the other door across from him, where the subway lines were diagramed. His eyes were shut throughout much of his song, squeezed so tightly that his Crow's feet were unnaturally deep. His voice carried with perfect clarity and the passion with which he sang was breathtaking.

When he was finished singing, we arrived at 135th St. He slid the guitar around and let it hang from his back. He picked up a small Bible and held it in his hands. He didn't open it, but he gripped it tightly.

"My brothers and sisters, I speak to you as a man who has wasted his life. I have used my years to seek pleasure from things that are temporary and destructive." There was a song-like consistency to his speech, and his accent was African. There was hardly an eye in the subway car not clearly fixated on this man, including mine.

"I have lived in a world of pornography, lust, and masturbation."

I was shocked at his words. Who admits to pornography in the public square? Who owns up to masturbation in front of strangers? These are topics that at best come out as joking references amongst friends, where it's safe to admit in vague fashion to such acts. And why in the world would he bare such shame in the first place. He invited stones to be cast upon him. Yet the cabin of passengers, myself included, was absorbed by this man's passion and sincerity. The train began to slow down near 116th St. This was my stop! But I could not physically move myself from this orator's grip. I found myself hanging onto his every word.

"I know the pain that comes from failing, from cheating, from living out lies. I am a nobody. But now, I am known by someone great!" A tear fell from his left eye. The train doors opened and then closed. I missed my stop and I did not care.

He might as well have been standing there naked, for he hid nothing of his soul. I wanted to break out, throw my arms up and pour out my failings too. Not so much to give him companionship, or even encouragement, but to gain a portion of the confidence and peace that was coming more clearly into his eyes.

"I am known by God, through his son Jesus Christ. Through him I have been given a new life, another chance. I offer this same peace of mind to you. I plead with you my brothers and sisters. Live no more a life of pain and hurt, find hope as I have!"

He swung his guitar around again and started another song. His chin lifted up and his voice rose to drown out the hum of the subway rails. Now eyes began to drift to the windows and around the passenger car, released in a way from the man's spell. I continued to study his every move.

He dressed in tattered corduroy pants and flip-flops, and his black shirt was stretched out around the neck the way it will when worn too many times without a good wash. But his passion and zeal were rare, as was his clarity of purpose. How could such a verbal concert proceed from this ragged physical image?

I was jealous of the confidence he had of his place in the world, in his present role in the human drama. My world, the path of medicine, is quite rigid. For a decade I knew each step that must be taken: undergraduate degree (four years), medical school (four years), and then residency (at least three years). Yet, in the subway car that day I had stumbled into a new place. My Bates physical exam book was in my lap, a book diagramming the mechanics of manipulating the human body to declare its diseases and deficiencies. It was my link to the world of medicine, but my heart was somewhere else. It was wrapped up in this man singing before me, and who, as far as I was concerned, sang only for me. He stood on the side of humanity, encompassing the human experience in its truest essence. What did medicine have to offer him? Had he gone to the doctor in the deepest throes of his sadness, he would have left in fifteen minutes with antidepressant pills. But he stood here now, singing and praising of a new life, filled with a desire to touch the lives of others in the same way. What if he had come to see me in clinic? Would I have brought healing? I just didn't know anymore.

Perhaps I was losing my passion for medicine. Or maybe, I didn't have a place in the world of medicine at all. Was I supposed to be the eye-in-the-sky, standing coolly by while calling out life saving algorithms over dying bodies? Was it in the ER, where patients come in and leave so fast, the names from one night are forgotten by the next? Was it in the operating theatre, where humans beings become little more than pumps and pipes to be tinkered on?

What I enjoyed was sitting down and talking to a patient. I wanted to talk about their family, their home, their culture, and their history. But for every patient there was a tome of dry medical science to read, there were checklists to complete, and there was a healthcare system to push them through. The energies required to accomplish those tasks siphoned off whatever passion was still lingering around after sitting and talking with a patient. Medicine was mechanical in that sense, but I was not a mechanic. Were I to ever stand up in front of my medical peers, I would cry out, "I have lived a life of studying things besides medicine, of pursuing interests outside of this classroom. I read newspapers and magazines and novels and learned foreign languages! I want to know people in the most intimate way, but I don't really care about knowing medicine!" That would be my soul-baring moment. The reality I was caught in was that medicine brought me closer to people and that's all I wanted. Was it worth the cost of years of indentured servitude? I guess I was in the middle of figuring that out.

I finally disembarked the subway. I wanted to embrace the Subway Evangelist and whisper into his ear, "Thank you." I got off the train without touching him but I stared at him until I left, hoping to give him a knowing glance that would at least say I was a kindred soul. But his eyes were still fixated on the opposite door. His voice carried in my ears above the echoing metal screech of the other trains in the hollow subway tube. Only the closing of the train doors sealed off his voice from the platform where I now stood. I watched as the train became smaller and smaller moving south into the dark hole of the New York City rail system.

Big Momma

Big Momma was the most entertaining, and bewildering, personality I came across during my two months at St. Luke's. Her presence filled every crevice on our floor, both for her demanding personality and for the enormity of her body. Her obesity was debilitating, requiring assistance in every facet of life. She could not even use the bathroom alone.

Big Momma was not even sick when she came onto our service. She showed up to us because another department had become so fed up with her. They slipped her through a bureaucratic loophole, as much as you can slip a 380 lb woman through anything, turfing her along to us. I really thought her sole purpose in the hospital was to have a team of highly trained medical personnel wipe her rear end.

In her gigantic electrical bed, specifically designed for the morbidly obese, she appeared very much like Jabba the Hutt. Talk of this resemblance brought smiles to the faces of all, and helped make her presence more tolerable. In her lap at all times of the day was a notebook, a typical Mead spiral, 70 sheets, college ruled. Whenever an action took place around her, the person performing the act was duly interrogated as to the purpose, the detail, the mechanics and the authority with which the act was performed. It was then duly noted in her spiral notebook.

I went in to visit her one morning and see how she was doing.

"And just what is your name?" Big Momma asked.

"Uh, Brian, ma'am." I replied. She began scribbling in her notebook.

"And what do you do here?" She asked.

"I'm a medical student." I said. "Actually, we've met before." Perplexed she put her head down and continued scribbling.

"And do you have a pager number that you can give me?" She asked.

"Oh yes, ma'am. Its 3-4654." I replied.

"Huh. And you are here to do what for me?" She asked.

"Well, I was just seeing…" I began.

"Actually, let me just tell you what you can do for me." She interrupted. "You can find out what's going on with my discharge. I was told yesterday morning that I would be discharged last night. And yet I'm here, now, talking to you. How do you explain that? Do you think that I deserve to be lied to that way? I'm beginning to think this is common practice in this hospital."

I wanted to reply in a broken and sheepish voice, "I'm just a bottom-dwelling, powerless medical student." Instead, I resorted to deflection, the modus operandi for any medical student on the hot seat. I reminded her that the attending went over with her last night the problem with her discharge: the outpatient care group had not yet agreed to take her. This was a sure bet to dissolve this argument since the whole team had an extensive discussion with her yesterday. She had taken notes like a court stenographer.

But in bringing up a past event I set off a scourge of back searching, not through her mind, but through her notebook. Frantically flipping page after page, I had challenged her authority, her intellect, and her book-keeping skills in one fell swoop. This was not to be tolerated.

"Well, I assure you that we did not have that conversation because I have no note of it here."

One of us was having a memory block. As sure as I was, I suddenly felt trapped in a pit next to this woman so eager to flick dirt onto my lifeless body. I paused to consider whether she was indeed correct. I was fortunate that yesterday's conversation was notable and curious enough that when Dr. Young, Brady, Viola, and I left her room we spent 10 minutes conferring on the peculiarity of her notebook and her persistent questions and scribbling.

"Are you sure you don't remember when Dr. Young, the attending physician here in charge of your care, came in and discussed your case with you? I was here with him too, and Dr. Charleston and Dr. Viola."

The disbelief on her face froze her for a moment. Her mouth stood open slightly, showing her white bottom teeth and a slight protrusion of her tongue. Her face was aimed slightly down, but her eyes rolled to the upper half of their orbit. They glared solidly into mine.

Broken clumps of dirt drizzled onto the back of my neck and shoulders. This was it. I wasn't making it out alive. My wife, my future children, and my once promising career in medicine were quickly becoming an effigy on a tombstone. If she stared at that slab of concrete as she was my corneas, she could have done the chiseling all by herself.

"What was your name again?" She asked.

There it was, she wanted to get the spelling right, for posterity's sake. I told her, but I wanted to scream that I was 'just a medical student, woman!'

"Go get me Dr. Young." She ordered. "I would like to speak with him myself. This treatment is unacceptable and I won't tolerate it. The entire staff here has been dismissing me since I got here. And now you're making me out a liar. You think you can treat your patients this way? Oh, no, no, no honey. Unacceptable. That is unacceptable!"

"Yes ma'am." I replied. Bahhhhhh, bahhhhhh. This would have been a more appropriate response given the sheepishness of my yes ma'am.

I scurried out and made a b-line for Brady who, thank goodness, was standing at the nurse's station talking on the phone.

"Dude. Dude, I need your help!" I said. He waved me with a calming o.k.

I was glad to talk to Brady of all people. His good humor was what I needed more than any words of comfort.

"Man, you just saw Big Momma, huh? I think she won, bro. What'd she say to you?" The smile on his face was reassuring in every way, because I realized that no matter what Big Momma said to Dr. Young or anybody else, I had an advocate for my cause. I told him everything that happened.

"Didn't I tell you not to go in there alone? You're not gonna win that battle. Jabba the Hutt, man. Don't forget that. Your Jedi mind tricks are useless on her!" At this we both laughed. "Don't worry about it. We just gotta get her out of here. We should put Pablo in charge of her. That would be awesome!"

In the way that only a very kind, upper-level resident can, I was redeemed from the pit of a malevolent patient. I had survived on a very short rope, empowered to practice medicine again, and even the better for it. Some patients had agendas that could never be satisfied. Addressing these agendas involves the art of medicine, not the science. The art of medicine is what keeps you from being buried alive, suffocated and ineffective for anything useful.

The Seal and the Fog

When I left New York City it was the first week of October. I left the way I had come, on the Chinatown bus. The return trip was very different, more that I was leaving something behind than envisioning forward. There was no longing to go back, only a strong sense that a significant portion of my life had just transpired and it was now sealed eternally by this excommunicating bus ride.

New York City reminded me that the universe was larger than me, and it was bigger than medicine too. Medicine was supposed to define my place on earth, but as I mistook vaginas for rectums and suffered under heavy handed patient agendas, where I fit in its paradigm had become less clear. What was I after, anyways? I longed to find a peace and purpose as I saw in the Subway Evangelist, and I always thought medicine would do that for me. Yet I was steadily diminishing in an expanding cosmos of daily demands and stress. My place in medicine became a fog before me, and I had nothing to do but keep walking through it.

Montana

Absarokee Arrival

I arrived in the middle of the night, less than a week since returning home to Shelley from New York City. My time home was rejuvenating but woefully short. The next month would be stretched even further since phone calls and emails would be my only contact with her.

The corridor leading from the America West gate in the Billings airport was carpeted green and conspicuously wide. It was landscaped for a people accustomed to open land. Space in Montana is a necessity of life, an element like fire, water, and air.

Along the walls were what seemed to be hieroglyphs of maps and scenic sketches tracing the journey of Lewis and Clark. Hieroglyphs were more familiar to me than these names and faces. The Northwest corner of the United States was a foreign land to me. And regarding the resident Native American peoples, I was shamefully oblivious.

Their history and culture, their beauty and their problems were far removed from where my interests had ever resided. That ignorance seeded a desire to know this land and her people, germinating into this month long elective in Family Medicine at the Indian Health Services Hospital in Crow Agency, Montana.

The tribe was Crow, known as Absarokee in their native tongue. They would take my ignorance of the North American Indians and bury it next to Custer on the banks of the Little Big Horn River. I would be thankful to be released of that burden.

I made my way down the double wide corridors and descended to the baggage claim to wait for my ride. All around were more images of the West and of the Indian. There were display cases with Indian jewelry, beadwork, and leather clothing.

After the baggage claim was emptied of travelers, I lay beside a mannequin showing off an outfit of sky blue denim and leather. It was sufficient cover to loiter through the night. My ride wasn't due until 7 o'clock in the morning. With me was the same luggage that I had traveled with to New York City, my home with adjustable straps. Using my JanSport backpack for a pillow, I settled in for a couple hours of airport sleep.

Just after 6:00 AM, voices and shuffling feet filled the baggage claim. I didn't move, hoping they'd disappear as fast as they'd come. Then the baggage belt four feet from my head began grinding along. I gathered my things and took a seat on a nearby bench and waited. An hour later my classmate and serendipitous companion for this trip picked me up. Her name was Melissa Dawalt.

Melissa is short and kept her blonde hair trimmed above her shoulders. Her frame was femininely compact and sturdy, consistent with her Midwestern roots. These roots were, more specifically, in Ohio which she could further prove by elevating the nasal intonation of her speech on command. Regardless of tone, her words came measured, preferring to listen as much as to speak.

I had only interacted with Melissa a few times in medical school. She signed up for the same rotation at Crow Agency, unbeknownst to either of us until three weeks before arrival. This was certainly a coincidence, but at the heart of it was a shared desire to work and live in a truly cross-cultural setting, even when restricted to the continental U.S. She knew as much about Crow Indians as I did, which wasn't much at all.

The Road to Crow

Billings holds the airport and everything else resembling urban life within the Montana state line. Melissa and I headed east on I-90 and within minutes were in the country. Beyond the window of our silver rental station wagon, the golden earth undulated in waves. In every direction land touched the sky like the sea. Montana is nicknamed *Big Sky* country and never have two words painted such a simple, yet marvelous picture of nature.

An hour later we crossed the Little Big Horn River at the Crow Agency interstate exit. Crow Agency serves as the municipal capital of the Crow Indian Reservation. First to greet us was a small gas and grocery store with a dilapidated Pepsi sign on the front awning. We drove past and through the outskirts of a decaying neighborhood. Houses were small and well-worn, to be kind. Nothing in the landscape spoke of Native American culture. There were surely no tee-pees to be found. Crow Agency could have been any poor, rural American town.

Exiting the neighborhood, we passed a large campground that centered on a larger than life rusted metal statue. A strong and lean Crow warrior sat atop his horse, ready for war. Fierce and proud, the forelegs of the horse kicked up towards the sky ready for battle. This statue provoked intimidation, the archetypal Native American in all his glory.

Continuing around the bend at the Little Big Horn Casino, we came upon the Crow Agency Public Health Service Indian Hospital. It is a two story structure of stacked tan and red brick. Dark pink columns guard the central entrance from which emanates three wings of the hospital. Built in 1995, it looked newer than anything on the reservation.

Our clerkship coordinator's office was located in back of the Optometry office. Behind the secretary's desk and the eye examining rooms was a title-less door passing into a two-person office. It was locked shut. Nobody responded to our knocks.

We turned to the secretary, "Is Nancy Breezepath available?" Melissa asked. That was the name of our coordinator.

The secretary, whose round youthful face was framed by long, straight jet black hair, responded, "Aw geez, she'll be around, can't say when though." She followed that statement with a friendly giggle.

"My name is Lynn. Why don't you sit down? Are you medical students?" She asked.

We told her we'd be around for the month shadowing the doctors in the clinic. Five minutes had not passed before we were behind the desk staring at a large map Lynn pulled out for us. She explained the layout of the reservation and the must-see places in and around Montana.

Lynn matched every ounce of our enthusiasm and curiosity. Either she was naturally that way, or she found our whiteness a curiosity of sorts. In any case, she mentioned her son played football for the local high school team, the Hardin Bulldogs.

"Why don't you come out to the game this Friday?" She offered.

"Lynn, you have no idea what you're saying. I love high school football!" I replied. That was very true, but before I could explain myself we heard a commotion within the Coordinator's office. We knocked again and were met by a sullen faced woman with light brown skin. It was Nancy Breezepath.

She offered no explanation for her tardiness and we were very soon passed off to her very nice, and very flaky, assistant Stephany for a hospital tour. In light of the connection we made with Lynn, Nancy's tardiness was a blessing in disguise. On our way out, I poked my head back into the Optometry office and whispered to Lynn, "See you on Friday."

War Bonnets and the Pink House

There were 24 inpatient beds and a large ambulatory care clinic, as well as a small Emergency Room. The facility was well-equipped with all the modern technological gadgets one would expect on American soil, including their own X-ray and ultrasound machinery. What gave it a distinct flavor was the Native American décor.

Embellishing every hallway were glorified photographs of great tribal chiefs, as well as modern social and political leaders of the Crow people. Even contemporary images showed a leader sitting upright on his horse wearing traditional Crow vestments, including the iconic War Bonnets. Large Eagle feathers swooped up and back, with colorful red and blue trim.

There were posters with the circle of life advertising help for alcohol abuse, a well known problem on all Indian reservations. Other posters campaigned against domestic violence, which goes hand-in-hand with alcohol abuse. One image in the outpatient clinic depicted the comforting of an abused Indian woman. Below read an empowering caption, "We have not lost Hope till the Hearts of our Women are on the Ground."

After our hospital tour, Stephany gave us directions to two places: the Pink House and the Custer battlefield. The Pink House was the hospital-owned duplex maintained for visiting students. The rent was a meager nine dollars a day. As for the battlefield, the hospital sat at the foot of the hill where Custer made his final stand. That became a priority of things to do while living on the Rez. But first we needed to settle in.

The Pink House was in the neighborhood we passed coming off the interstate. It sat on a side street amidst many other duplexes, though none more vibrant than our very pink house. Melissa stayed in the right half, I stayed in the left.

The apartment was carpeted and well heated, with a television and telephone. I had a cell phone with me but only one company had towers this side of Hardin, the nearest town 20 miles away. That company wasn't mine. The Pink House otherwise provided a civilized existence for me, a step up from Maria's apartment and the youth hostel in Manhattan.

Resident Encyclopedia

We made our way to the hospital around 8:30 AM every morning. We usually hit-up the Native Grounds espresso stand located outside the main hospital parking lot. It was a small stand painted an array of yellow and red vertical stripes with barely enough room for the server inside. The Arab muffin-guy in New York City had a mobile home compared to this fellow.

But what the Indian lacked in size, he made up for in flare. Loud tribal music blasted off vinyl next to the espresso machine, which he broadcast on FM radio. Within 30 feet of the stand we could hear thumping tribal music from the confines of our silver hatchback.

My role at Crow was to shadow the Family Medicine doctors in the various settings offered at the hospital. This included general outpatient clinics and the Emergency Room. Shadowing a Family Physician was usually quite boring. The medical student eavesdrops on a conversation weeks, months, or even years old. It is the physician's rapport with the patient that guides the visit. That is the value of the specialty, and a student can hardly experience that continuity of patient care during a one-month clerkship.

During my first clinic shift Tuesday morning, I worked with a silver haired, Midwestern doctor who went by Dr. J. He seemed far too enamored with having a medical student around. He threw out assignments for me to follow-up on various medical facts, but his teaching points often contradicted the textbooks. He was in the process of studying for his boards, though he'd been practicing Family Medicine for decades. It was all quite suspicious. He also talked in the third person to patients which grated my ears like fingernails on a chalkboard.

"Now, Mrs. Pretty-Weasel, you're gonna take the medicine like Dr. J asked, aren't you?" He would say. "Dr. J doesn't like it when his patients don't take his medicine." I wanted to hurl.

The next afternoon I came into clinic to meet up with Dr. Joyce. She was a spunky redhead whose previous career was in Veterinary Medicine. She dressed like a city girl, with hairspray, heavy makeup and tall black leather boots to match her black skirt. None of which hinted at treating animals or working on a rural Montana Indian reservation.

She was standing at the edge of the long nursing station desk talking to another of the clinic doctors. I approached her as the man walked away. She leaned over to me and asked in a quiet voice, "Have you met Dr. Roberts?"

I had not, but I had heard of him. He was something of a superstar on the Rez. Every clinic, every hospital department, every conglomeration of practicing physicians has their resident en-vivo encyclopedia. Dr. Roberts was that person at Crow Agency. As Dr. Joyce said to me at the nursing station, "If he doesn't know it, either it isn't known, or it isn't worth knowing."

A white man wholly grafted into the Crow nation, Dr. Roberts worked at Crow Agency before he entered the field of medicine. He did a Medicine & Pediatrics combined residency (known in the profession as Med-Peds) at that grandiose hospital-in-the-sky known as Massachusetts General Hospital, Harvard's historic teaching hospital. But you wouldn't know that from Dr. Roberts, even if you asked him directly.

His jaw line was tight and stoic and his body thin. While he was clearly intense in his drive, he was not one with nervous energy. He did not pace, he did not speak rapidly. He emanated an attitude of calmness. In the tethered chaos of Indian bureaucracy, I found him to be the glue of the clinic, and our clerkship.

I worked with Dr. Joyce throughout the morning. She taught me a strangle hold leg lock maneuver to evaluate low back pain, a trick she no doubt learned as a veterinarian and not in medical school. After playing Twister on the exam room table, the patient and I both agreed I would learn this better another day.

After morning clinic I met up with Melissa at the hospital's small three-table cafeteria. In this small room there was a counter window leading back to the kitchen. We took our food from a Crow with a mesh nylon skull cap and sat down across from a table of Caucasian nurses.

"The docs are pretty cool here, don't you think?" Melissa asked.

"They're a ragtag bunch of personalities," I replied, "and they've all got a story about how they ended up here."

"I think they're all here for the loan payback." She said.

She was referring to the Indian Health Service's physician recruitment program. This federal program offers a package of salary, debt repayment, and other perks in exchange for a minimum two year commitment to work on a reservation. There are similar programs for nurses as well.

I leaned in towards Melissa, inadvertently dumping the bell of my stethoscope into the ketchup on my tray. The only other mistake I did more frequently than this one was leaning over to pick up a fallen pen, only to watch all the pens in my breast coat pocket tumble onto the ground.

"Anyways," I began in a low voice while grabbing for a pile of napkins. "Is it weird that all the docs and nurses are white?" Look back in the kitchen, they're all Crow."

Melissa acknowledged this statement without turning to look, nodding with her eyes closed as though agreeing to an undisputed fact. "It's pretty segregated here." She said. "All the staff jobs are Crow."

"Have you seen a Crow physician or nurse?" I asked.

"I don't know if that exists," she replied.

I never met a Native American physician in the outpatient clinic, or anywhere else in the hospital. Crow natives filled out the non-medical staff of clerks, janitors, cooks, and the like. Essentially, any position requiring higher education was filled by bright- skinned Caucasian outsiders. Melissa and I began to sense the social role we inadvertently came here and filled.

Differences in skin tones around the hospital were enhanced by an equally glaring verbal contrast. The nurses' English chatter in the cafeteria broke up the Crow tongues and clanging dishes in the kitchen. Crow Indians still spoke their native language.

"What about the patients?" Melissa asked. "What have you been seeing?"

"Lot of diabetes, and about every last patient is overweight!"

"I agree!" Melissa raised both hands to count off her fingers, "I've seen diabetes, heart disease, high blood pressure, and more than one alcoholic. These aren't rare diseases. Every one of them can be prevented, easy."

"The alcohol is a big problem." I replied. "Isn't the reservation dry?"

"Yeah, so was my college campus. Please." Melissa sighed. "The saddest thing I saw was a young girl with Meth Mouth. Her front teeth were disgusting, all eroded and off color."

"And this in spite of free health care." I replied.

For all the promises the Federal Government has broken towards Native Americans, health care delivery is one area of tremendous success. Federal tax dollars have built a comprehensive system of hospitals and clinics spanning the entire Indian nation, of which the Crow hospital is a part. Their health insurance even allows referrals to outside specialists, although wait lists can average six months or more. This socialized medical scheme is free to all Crow, whether they live on the reservation or not.

Melissa noticed the clock on the wall showed we were in danger of running late to our afternoon clinic session. "We'd better go." She stated, gathering her orange tray. "Let's see if this morning was a fluke."

Unfortunately, that afternoon and every day thereafter only reinforced our first impressions. Grossly overweight men and women came in and out of those hospital doors suffering from a plethora of preventable disease. Other consequences surfaced as well, like a significant domestic violence problem fueled by the rampant alcoholism. The Native Americans suffered from damaging individual choices and cultural behaviors. Ultimately, my month at Crow Agency was a window into this discrepancy of available health care and atrocious health status.

Friday Night Lights

The invitation to watch the Hardin Bulldogs varsity football team play under Friday night lights excited me all week. On the LOTIL, high school football is #7.

I played high school football, and as a teenage boy, it was my life. My closest friends and my fondest memories are all wrapped up with football. I experienced the pain of defeat and the joy of victory, losing and then winning our Division Championship my junior and senior year, respectively.

Not that it was all glory. I hated practice with a passion. Sitting in fifth period class, I watched the clock incessantly, dreading the moment I had to walk towards the locker room to get ready for practice. Monday practices were especially terrible as they finished with wind sprints and weight lifting until well after dark.

If I had not become a physician, I would have coached high school football. Before my acceptance to medical school I was searching for teaching jobs in south Louisiana with that goal in mind. But I was too curious about the world, sure that I needed to experience the world to understand it. What could I share with young people if I myself was still seeking understanding?

Besides the football, this Friday night event was a chance to meet Lynn around her family and her people, experiencing life the way they did. The only way to know a people is to share an experience within the boundaries of their world.

The game was in Hardin, a town built around the economy of an interstate exit. Melissa and I had gone there previously only to buy groceries. Darkness had fallen when we got to the game. Parking was filled to overflowing so we had to walk a fair distance.

Energy burned from the night air as we approached the field. I could smell the innocent competition, the naïve acceptance from everyone that tonight we lived and died by the battle on the field. I wanted to sprint to those silver stands.

Before the entrance was a grill sizzling with hot dogs and hamburgers. The smell made me salivate. I held off though, not wanting to carry a plate of food and drink while finding our seats. Unable to convince the ticket lady that Melissa and I were really students, even owing hundreds of thousands of dollars in medical student loans, we paid full price and entered the stadium.

We approached the base of the stands when I stopped Melissa with a tap on her shoulder. I preferred to look for Lynn from there, before stepping into full view of the crowd. If I was going to enter that crowd, I needed to be purposeful about it. But the view was slanted and obscured so Melissa started climbing the steps. I hesitated, a warm rush of anxiety swimming right through me, quickening my pulse and throwing it into my throat.

I abhorred the idea of staring at every unknown face in the crowd, and receiving back those same stares. Whether it was the first day of a college class, entering a conversation in the basement of a Manhattan hostel, or staring at a crowd of high school football fans, I always have to overcome inertia before making that initial impact with people. For some reason, anonymity, which I quite enjoy, does not give me cover. Only when I know the people, or am known by them, is there no anxiety.

Reluctantly, I followed Melissa, whose easy gaze and confident stride did not share my anxiety, nor did they glance back to see if I was coming along. I climbed up after her to the base of the aluminum stands scanning the crowd for Lynn, becoming a visual obstacle to a whole section of Hardin Bulldog fans. My anxiety gave way as Lynn's smiling face sat right there in front of us. We clamored to the empty space she had saved for us to her left. She had blankets for us too, so our rear ends wouldn't freeze on the cold, grainy benches.

She introduced us to everyone around her. There were sisters, brothers, aunts, uncles, cousins, second cousins, and persons currently or formerly married to members of her family.

They were young and old, infantile and senile. For my family, this would have been a reunion seen once every decade. For Lynn, it was another Friday night. She barely acknowledged them apart from introducing me or pointing them out.

To Lynn's right sat a quiet man who wore a plain baseball cap and a flannel hunting jacket. He had a round, tan face and a moustache.

"This is Norman, my husband." Lynn leaned back and Norman leaned over extending his hand to me, then to Melissa. He didn't offer many words, though his greeting was warm. The game had already started so the focus was aimed at the field.

"That's Jeremy, my son, right there on the sidelines in that crowd of boys, number 32. He doesn't play much on Varsity."

I asked Lynn for her game program to help me follow the action on the field. She handed me an orange sheet of paper with the players' number, name, height, weight and year. This list was humorous for the many Indian names. One of the more interesting names was Lynn's son, #32, White-Man-Runs-Him.

"How come #32 is not Morrison?" I asked Lynn, who's last name was Morrison.

"My maiden name is White-Man-Runs-Him. Norman and I have only been married for seven years. We don't have any kids of our own. I had Jeremy when I was 18, and Arlis was born two years later. But the oldest is Nathaniel. I got pregnant with him when I was 15!" She chuckled at this. It was a laugh of humility, knowing that her story exposed faults and mistakes, but comfortable with her past all the same. Plus, she just liked to laugh.

She proceeded to tell us her story of being pregnant when she was young and going off to college only to get pregnant again. Now I realized how young she did look for being a mother of three kids. She was only 36 years old. She was overweight, but you could tell she was active, even athletic.

It was getting colder by the quarter. I joked with Norman, who still had not said much, about how rough this was on a southerner from Louisiana, "You know, they say in Louisiana that winter falls on a Thursday."

Norman smiled. Accepting my overture, he leaned over so that we hovered over Lynn's lap.

"Here in Montana there are only three seasons," he said, "last winter, this winter, and next winter!"

Norman opened up now. He listened intently to others, but once he got to talking, he went on and on. I didn't mind though, on account of his excellent sense of humor. He wasn't one to laugh at his own jokes. He let his punch lines sit in the air and affect you the way they did, but with a knowing gleam in his eye that he just said something worthy of a laugh.

We talked for most of the first half. The game became obsolete in my mind, though I was still energized by the atmosphere. This atmosphere framed the impression of my conversations with Lynn and Norman.

I asked Lynn to tell me the story behind the name White-Man-Runs-Him.

"My Great-Great-Grandfather had another name when he was a little kid, but he was always sick. The Crow have this belief that if you change somebody's family or name, you can heal their sickness. So he was thrown away by his family. Another family took him in but they didn't adopt him.

"There was a white trapper who used to come around to trade with the Indians, and he always brought his son with him. One time some Crow boys were outside playing when the Trapper and his son came around. They decided to play a mean trick on this little white boy. He got so mad! He chased the Crow boys in anger. For some reason he mostly chased White-Man-Runs-Him. So they changed his name. And you know, it must have helped with his sickness too because he lived a long, long time."

To my Anglo-Saxon ears these Indian names were comical. They were vivid descriptions of the world they experienced. Hearing this story, I saw that names carried pride, even healing power. My amusement changed into envy at having such a name.

Lynn continued, "He got famous because he was a scout for Custer and one of the few survivors of the Battle of Little Big Horn. I think the others were Curley and Harry Moccasin. But, White-Man-Runs-Him interacted with Custer himself. Because of how long he lived they interviewed him a lot and always asked him to tell the story of the battle with Custer. But they made him dress up for this and take pictures. He hated all that and didn't want to talk or think about what happened that day. He just wanted to move on."

I was intrigued by this Custer scout. The Battle of Little Bighorn, fought in June of 1876, was a devastating, even embarrassing, loss by the American Army in their burgeoning war against the entire Indian Nation. All 210 men of General George A. Custer's Seventh Calvary were killed in a miscalculated attempt to surprise the encampment of the Lakota chief, Sitting Bull. The Crow were providing scouts, like White-Man-Runs-Him, for Custer's efforts.

Portrayed as a massacre in the American newspapers, Custer became a legend and the battle a rally call to stiffen up the fight against the 'savage' Native American tribes. Within a year of the great Indian victory, all participating tribes had come to surrender to the U.S. Army.

"Aren't ya'll ashamed that you fought with the white man against other Indians?" I asked Lynn.

Norman leaned back in and replied, "If a Crow walks into a bar full of Sioux, even today, he'd better leave before the door shuts behind him. He might not make it out walking." His eyes looked playfully serious.

Norman continued, "Listen, the Crow were enemies of all the Indian tribes way before the white man. We were fighting all the time; they wanted our land. When the white man came, the Crow were expecting them. They had seen them coming in dreams. They knew they were here to stay, too. So we fought with them to fight our enemies, our common enemies. And look today, our reservation is Crow land. You know what they say about Custer's Last Stand: The Cheyenne fought it, the Sioux got the credit, and the Crow got the land. We're the only tribe still on our original land. We didn't get moved here, we've always been here."

The crowd roared as a Hardin running back made a long gain. This re-entry to the present startled me. I had lost myself in Norman's words. Actually, it was not his words so much as the pride with which he spoke. There was a change in his voice when he spoke of the Crow people. His words were heavier and landed harder on my ears. It was not hubris, only affection for those who had passed their blood on to him.

I learned later about the dream that foresaw the white man's coming. It was Plenty-Coups, the last Crow chief to know life before the white man, who made those prophecies. He transitioned the Crow, and the entire Indian nation, from the old life to the new. This happened around the turn of the 20th century.

Plenty-Coups was a young boy when he had his dream. In a quest likened to Moses on Mt Sinai or Jesus in the Judean wilderness, Plenty-Coups journeyed to the peak of what the Crow called the Crazy Mountains. There he fasted for three days hoping to receive his *Medicine*, the spiritual power that accompanied a Crow through war and peace.

If he was blessed, he'd be approached by an animal that would speak his future and impart his medicine. Plenty Coups even chopped off the tip of his left index finger as a desperate call for *Helpers* to visit and aid him in his spiritual quest. The result was the visit in a dream by a Man-person dressed in Buffalo robe.

He stood with the Man-person who shook a red rattle made from a dried animal bladder. Shaking the rattle called forth from a hole in the ground legions of buffalo. They filled the open Montana plain until it was black. In a flash, they were gone again, as fast as they had come. Again more animals came and filled the plain, but they were not buffalo. They were strange four-legged animals that ate the grass and bellowed in a way unlike the buffalo. They were spotted in color.

Confused, the vision's climax came as Plenty-Coups was shown a dark forest. The Four Winds gathered their strength and attacked the forest, demolishing all but one lone tree. In that tree was the lodge of the Chickadee. A voice explained to him how this animal was least in strength but strongest of mind. He gained wisdom by listening well and learning from the mistakes of others.

When the ten-year old Plenty-Coups returned home, he spoke his dream to the medicine-men. Yellow-bear, in whose lodge the ceremony took place, explained the meaning of Plenty Coups' dream, "...the white men will take and hold this country and their Spotted-buffalo [Cows] will cover the plains." He continued, "The Four Winds represent the white man and those who will help him in his wars. The forest of trees is the tribes of these wide plains. And the one tree that the Four Winds left standing after the fearful battle represents our own people, the Absarokees [Crow], the one tribe of the plains that has never made war against the white man...After the battle of the Four Winds he still held his home, his country, because he had gained wisdom by listening to the mistakes of others and knew there was safety for himself and his family." [1]

This dream led the Crow spiritually and practically through the great upheaval of white European settlement. Lynn knew Plenty-Coups' dream because she had read his famous biography by Frank B. Linderman. Her mother also passed down the story

1 Linderman, F.B. (1930). *Plenty-coups: Chief of the crows*. Lincoln, NE: University of Nebraska Press.

as she learned it from a very old Crow woman named Nappy White Arm. The vision was still being carried by Crow people.

We were interrupted again, this time by a Hardin touchdown. I decided to digest what I just heard, as well as a hamburger. I walked down to the grill I had passed earlier. My heart dropped to see they were cleaning up and the grill was already gone. I asked the lady cleaning up if there was any food left.

"Oh, honey, yeah. Take this plate and get whatever you want over there on the back of that truck." I turned around and saw tubs of macaroni salad, hamburgers, and coleslaw sitting in disposable aluminum pans on the cab of a red pick-up truck. When I got closer I saw sheets of brownies for dessert. My heart soared, as eating for free and macaroni salad are #12 and #13, respectively on the LOTIL.

I asked for an extra plate and loaded down both. Carefully I returned to my seat, drawing stares from everyone I passed. I felt some kinship now to the crowd, so there was no hint of anxiety as I passed through. They were at least known to me.

"It's for a bunch of people," I whispered to those I made eye-contact with. Lynn and Norman cracked up when they saw my plates of food.

I was chewing on a mouthful of macaroni salad and basking in the electric atmosphere when I overheard Lynn say to Norman, "I couldn't believe he said that to his own brother-in-law..."

The statement as retold by Lynn was one of sarcasm. It was at the brother-in-law's expense, but it was nothing malignant. I found it peculiar that Lynn went on about it. I finally interrupted her, "Why such a big deal that he poked fun at this guy?"

Norman leaned over and said, "It's his brother-in-law. In Crow culture, a brother cannot joke or do anything taken as an insult to his brother-in-law. A brother-in-law must be held in the highest regard."

"Why is that relationship so special?" I asked.

Lynn replied in her typical way, "Aw gees, how do we know!" She was already chuckling. Unlike Norman, Lynn did laugh at her own jokes. That's what made everything she said funny.

Norman added, "Oh, yeah man, the Crow have some crazy traditions with their families. You know another one? Mother-in-laws and son-in-laws can't talk to each other. They can't even sit at the same table. Some people are real strict about it. They won't even sit in the same house."

I was astonished. I asked Norman, "Do you talk to Lynn's mom?"

"We don't do all those things our parents did." He replied. "But we're careful by it."

I went back to my burger, and we all gave our attention back to the game. Halftime came and went and so did the second half. Hardin lost in the last few minutes of a nail-biter. The crowd was dejected. The players shook hands in midfield like opposing centipedes brushing past each other. The smoke rising from their de-helmeted heads gave the night air a sense of enchantment.

On the way out, Melissa and I saw five or six different people from the hospital. In a week's time we had developed a semblance of community in Montana. I already felt more connected than I ever did in New York City. This was small town living at its best.

Public Health on the Rez

I made great efforts to understand what Public Health infrastructure exists in the Indian Health Service. The closest thing to a Public Health director at Crow Agency was Carol Wildhair, the politically appointed (read: relative of tribal chairman) Director of the Crow Tribal Health Department. She graciously sat with me in her tiny office adjacent to the Big Horn Casino. She made it clear that no official Public Health professional worked to promote health or prevent disease on this or any other Indian reservation.

Her department did manage to put on a 74-mile *Heart of Crow Country Walk* within the 1.5 million acre Crow Indian Reservation. It was a relay walk to generate enthusiasm for physical exercise and to show anyone could walk a mile. 1500 Crow citizens participated. I watched the video that proved it. I was encouraged and devastated all at once.

People were excited to feel the warmth of the sun and the cool brush of Montana wind. But the number of obese men, women, and children was awe-inspiring. Every cheek that smiled on camera was plump with layers of subcutaneous fat. This was a tribe that once consisted of men who ran afoot with horses, and women who carried families across the Western plains. Now, there was no semblance of that people, not even a remnant.

The etiology of the epidemic was terrible eating habits in the context of a sedentary lifestyle. The Crow people fill up on fry bread tacos, a local favorite, fast food, chips, and sodas. Even the traditional diet dripped with beef and fat. That was suitable for a man laboring in the sun to survive, and for whom war was a seasonal sport, but the genetic balance of the Native American had not transitioned to the new way, and so these diseases devastated them.

Still seeking a deeper understanding, I sought out the Public Health nurses. The name hints at a role akin to Public Health officers, but their job is actually to make home visits across the reservation. That was not the population perspective I was hoping to gain.

Nevertheless, I joined up with a white woman named Ruth who'd been working at Crow for the better part of twenty years. Like many whites, she was from the surrounding area and saw her involvement with the Indians as an opportunity for interesting work.

We drove out to Lodge Grass, a town 30 minutes from Crow Agency. This small community consisted of a few neighborhoods, all of them dilapidated. There was a supermarket and a school of the same quality.

We pulled into a large dirt parking lot in front of a solitary trailer home. A young, overweight woman greeted us shyly from behind the cracked door. She couldn't have been a day older than twenty.

Ruth returned her greeting with a warm smile that had somehow, over her fifty years of life, maintained a simple naiveté. "How are you today, Jessica?" Ruth asked.

She answered shyly that she was doing well then disappeared behind the door. She left it open, which we took as our invitation to enter.

I took great care walking into that trailer as junk was splayed out everywhere. Walls were covered with pictures of Disney characters and other childish décor. Papers were strewn across every elevated surface. Dirty cups, plates, and silverware littered the tabletops. Cheerios were spilt over the kitchen counter. A long strip of sticky tape hung down from the ceiling to the level of my shoulders. It swayed gently back and forth as the numerous flies caught in its grasp struggled for their lives.

In the living room, mismatching couches held a five year old boy and an infant lying on his back staring at the ceiling. Everything in the room, including the little boy, was pointed to a television airing a daytime talk show.

Like the boy, I was transfixed by the amazing speech radiating from the television. There were so many beeps blocking particular words that at times entire sentences were dropped. I was frightened to think this young boy passed his entire day this way. His brain knew only to soak in every stimulus and to mold itself accordingly. I asked Jessica to turn off the television.

Ruth asked me to examine the baby boy. She needed his vital signs and a quick run through his cardiac and respiratory systems. I had not expected this request. Earlier she had only mentioned taking the baby's height and weight, and talking with the mother about immunizations.

Noticing the perplexed look on my face, she lowered her voice and said, "I can't tell a murmur from a watermelon. Been trying for twenty-five years! Just listen to her, you're the doctor."

It was not the request Ruth made that perplexed me. It was the expectation that I could fulfill it. She flashed that naïve smile again. Goodness, how did she maintain such innocence through all these years?

I sat on the edge of the couch and leaned over the baby. Ruth was in the kitchen talking to the mom. Neither of them paid attention to me.

I stared down at the baby and spoke softly, "Listen, I'm new at this but I promise I'll do my best, O.K.? Now, stare blankly at the ceiling if you want to continue with this examination." Baby affirmed, so I placed my stethoscope on his chest.

I listened with more intensity than I had ever mustered for a simple heart auscultation. I had never been in the situation where my word stood. In fact, no one in my four years of clinical training had ever sought my opinion...for anything! If there was a pathologic murmur, it was for me to find. If I didn't catch it, the problem might present itself when it was too late. In a manner of speaking, this baby's life was in my hands.

My palms and forehead moistened. I was plagued by a desire for more experience under my belt. But experience was a heinous thing. To attain it, I had to go forward without it.

I listened long and hard and heard nothing abnormal, no swoosh of a murmur or extra heart sounds, just the typical lub-dub of a healthy heart. I palpated the abdomen and did a few other maneuvers until I trusted this baby was in good health. I got up and walked over to Ruth and Jessica.

"The baby looks good." I told them both. "But I remind you that I'm just a medical student." This was my standard qualifier absolving me from all responsibility. "It's important that he sees a Family doc at Crow. And he definitely needs to get his vaccinations." The mother was still very quiet, but she nodded subtly in agreement.

Ruth continued their conversation as we headed for the door, "So you've been at IGA for three months now, right?" IGA was the grocery store in Lodge Grass.

Jessica affirmed and added, "It's been tough this last week, having to watch the baby."

There was emotional distance when she said "the baby." That took me off-guard. "Is that not your baby?" I asked.

"No, well, he's not my child anymore." She replied.

I stared blankly at her, then at Ruth. I was obviously missing something.

"Jessica gave him away to her Aunt." Ruth finally spoke up. "It was too difficult to raise the baby and to work full time. But the Aunt is sick and in the hospital. So she's baby-sitting."

"So, you're babysitting your own baby?" I asked.

Jessica nodded her head. She didn't offer an explanation, so I didn't press for one.

As we drove off the dirt parking lot I asked Ruth, "Will she ever get her child back?"

"No, no. Jessica can never take the child back. He's not hers anymore. She sees him a lot; the Aunt lives here in Lodge Grass." Ruth continued on about other peculiarities of life amongst the Indians, as well as her obsession with the practice of swaddling and shushing newborn infants. She never really addressed the issue of giving children away. This issue needed explanation directly from a Crow.

Tribal Mechanics

Back in the clinic, I worked with some new doctors. Dr. Byron was a Christian man with a pony tail. In the straight laces of the rural West this haircut was the remnant of a rebellious past, or at least a very free spirit. He was also pro-gay marriage, a stance not readily shared by America's Christian politick.

I also spent some time shadowing Dr. Upchurch, the resident general surgeon of the hospital. He was quick to clarify, "I am a Family Physician who does surgeries." It was equally clear that over the last twenty years he had removed as many appendixes and gall bladders as any surgeon in Billings. His energy was way too high for standard outpatient medical practice, and was otherwise expended on surgery or outdoor activities.

While working through my clinic days, important questions arose about the logistics of my rotation. Mainly, the promised travel reimbursement as part of the rotation. The U.S. government recruited even us medical students to the reservation, hoping to create enthusiasm for returning later as physicians.

Nancy Breezepath, however, was nowhere to be found. I asked every staff member, including her assistant, Stephany, "Where did my coordinator go?" I was answered with blank stares. She told nobody where she was going. She transferred no decision making capacity to her assistant.

Such action had nothing to do with legacy, as it had with Anderson, the Columbia medical student. It was something far worse: complacency. Complacency spawned from a lack of competition and the inability to usurp power from positions entrenched by blood relations. Nancy Breezepath's management style was the result of such a tribal bureaucracy. Needing guidance within this maze, I turned to a white man. Dr. Roberts quickly became the de facto coordinator of my clerkship experience.

Melissa and I visited Dr. Roberts late one afternoon. We explained to him our dilemma. Dr. Roberts was wholly unsurprised by the absence of our coordinator. He did however shed some light on the situation.

"It's ingrained inefficiency." He said. "They hand out hospital positions to members of the tribe. As long as your tribe is in power, you have your job."

The inefficiencies allowed of government Indian Health Service workers are like some immovable scar on the landscape. Individually poor performance is shrouded time and again by a clan-based system of tribal politics. In such a system, substandard work finds impunity amongst the leadership in power. Family member hires family member. If the person was never hired for the skills or education they possessed, why be fired for underwhelming performance?

Lynn had also once enlightened me on the power of this clan based socio-political structure. There were ten clans in the Crow tribe: Whistling Water, Bad War Deeds, Greasy Mouth, Sorelip Lodges, Big Lodge, Newly Made Lodge, Piegan, Filth Eaters, Ties the Bundle, and Brings Game Without Shooting. The power players of these clans had a tight grip on the people. They could, and would, hold your paycheck if you did not attend their political rallies during election season. And if a new party won the election for Chairman, a complete transfer of jobs swept across the reservation.

Incidentally, it was election season at Crow that October. Melissa and I had visited a political rally by the great warrior statue. There were many speeches that night, though we didn't understand a word. They spoke only in Crow. We did eat the hot dogs and cheap tubs of potato salad, the kind sold at Sam's Club.

Dr. Roberts continued clarifying the tribal mess within the hospital. "We've known for a long time that our billing system at the hospital is inefficient. We could recoup millions more by billing insurance companies more efficiently. But when external auditors came, they were turned away. Crow officials saw it as an insult. And they understood the money that could be gained."

It was painstakingly clear that tribal politics were cause for much of the inferior healthcare, education, and financial poverty on the reservation. I wondered aloud to Dr. Roberts why outsiders like him could not guide these people to a better future.

"Whites cannot fix the problem, Brian." He said. "We're too much a part of the problem."

Understanding this balance of tribal Native American culture surviving in a sea of Western civilization required more perspective. I now had two big topics needing clarification from a Native American. That is exactly what I would seek from my closest Crow companions, Lynn and Norman.

The Battlefield

Melissa and I left that meeting frustrated and disheartened. Our somber mood led us to visit the Little Bighorn Battlefield, site of Custer's famous last stand. We took a left at the exit of the hospital and drove the one and a half minutes up the hill to the battlefield site.

The lay of the land was striking. The Little Bighorn River, known as the Greasy Grass River by Native Americans, meandered in the valley below surrounded by banks of trees and bush. October leaves painted the landscape in bright strokes of orange and yellow. The hills were plentiful and rolled across the horizon.

The battlefield was remarkable for its simplicity. The slope of one solitary yellow grass hill contained an uncoordinated distribution of small, grey tombstones. With only a black background distinguishing his tombstone, General George Armstrong Custer's grave humbly marked the spot where he fell on June 25, 1876.

It is not often that a nation commemorates the actual spot where a man shed his blood and breathed his last. But Custer was in the right place and the right time to be killed and to be remembered. For most that would be a vicious combination; for a military officer it was a glorious fate. His death took on a greater meaning than his life. This is why people still come by the thousands, year after year, to see where the course of American history took an irrevocable turn in his honor.

Carcass Sweat

The following Saturday Lynn and Norman invited Melissa and me to go day-camping in the Big Horn Mountains. Non-Crow were prohibited from entering this area of the reservation without permission and accompaniment by a local Crow. Norman arranged everything for our visit.

Originally, we had hoped to go Buffalo hunting. A bluff in this mountain range contains the reservation's 200 buffalo, also known as American Bison. One small fence hems in the Buffalo while the rest of the border is a sheer drop off into the canyon below. It is a natural holding pen.

Buffalo hunting is a touchy issue on the reservation. You have to be Crow and have a permit and guide. We had only one of three, so we elected to day-camp in the canyon below the range.

From the highway view, the landscape was yellow and green and vacuous. There were houses here and there, but most were barely visible from the road. As we drove along, Lynn and Norman seemed to repeat the same phrases, "That house over there, that's my cousin...." or "that's my brother's land..." They were related to everyone.

Norman pointed out the home of his step-uncle, Ivan Small. "When Ivan lived down on Muddy Creek, he had a daughter who traveled down to Mexico and brought back some jalapeño peppers. She made her dad some burritos with those jalapeño peppers and old Ivan ate three of them the next morning for breakfast. It was winter at the time, below zero weather with snow on the ground. Ivan saddled his horse and headed out to check his cows as he was a rancher. He had ridden out a mile or two when he felt a terrible urge to poop. He realized he wouldn't be able to ride home in time so he went to the bathroom right there in that field.

'It was hot coming out' he said, on account of those jalapeño peppers from Mexico. Three days later he was out checking those cows again when he witnessed quite a sight. The snow had melted around that poop and there were two coyotes warming their hands next to it!" That was typical for Norman. He was always in the midst of telling a joke, even when he seemed completely serious.

Norman's zeal for telling jokes was matched in symbiotic harmony by Lynn, who lived on the precipice of laughter. Jokes weren't even necessary to get her going. I would turn around in the car and stare at her, like what Pablo did to Brady on morning rounds at St. Luke's. A few seconds of not breaking my gaze and she'd fall into her bubbly 'hee, hee, hee'. This giggle was always followed by a deep inhalation, and then rounded out with an exhaled, "Aw, shoot." It was predictable and fun. Lynn has a very happy soul.

Stopping at a small IGA grocery store for picnic supplies and food we came across fathers, brothers, uncles, and half-cousins. Our trip was only miles old and had covered every potential branch a family tree could sprout. Lodge Grass was the last area of consolidated population we saw on our way to the campground. Maybe now we'd quit running into family members.

I was sitting in the front passenger seat of the big red F-250 when I finally broached the subject I had longed to discuss. I told them about Jessica giving away her baby.

"Oh, yeah," Norman replied. He said it drawn out and nasally, like the accent of a West-Coast Mexican-American. "That's what we do here. If you can't take care of your kid, you give 'em away. We take care of each other like that."

Norman continued, "It happened to me. The family I grew up in, they took me from my mother!"

Norman's mother went out of town for two weeks to visit his dying grandmother. Norman stayed with his mom's cousin, Tom and Suzie Morrison. They were a ranching family and better off financially than Norman's family. When Norman's mom came home, the Morrison's wanted to keep him. They had no children of their own and, in particular, no sons. This made life very difficult for a rancher.

Norman's mom was horrified at the idea. She refused at first, but was pressured by the elders of the family. She gave him up with tears in her eyes. Norman was only one year old.

"The ironic thing is that I grew up poor anyways. They ended up having too many kids and too many mouths to feed." He said.

Norman did receive a small inheritance from the Morrison family. He used it to buy their current house on the reservation.

He continued, "When I divorced my first wife, my Dad took my five year old son. I couldn't do anything to stop it. I could visit him, and I did, but I couldn't do anything to get him back. I couldn't overcome the old man's will." Norman's son always felt abandoned during that time. The boy was twelve years old when he was finally returned home after Norman's dad became demented.

Lynn also suffered the stripping away of children. After the birth of her third child, Arlis, she needed to return to Missoula where she had studied for a time. Missoula was only a few hours west of the reservation.

Lynn's father sat her down and said, "You can take the little one, but the rest are staying here."

He was not without reason. He understood that Lynn's youth and the sheer number of kids without a male figure in the house would be overwhelming. But he wasn't talking about babysitting these kids. They would be permanently raised by him and his wife. Lynn would be like a close Aunt.

Lynn did leave, but only for a short time. Her return to the reservation was emotionally difficult by having her children so close but not living with her. After some years, and after meeting and marrying Norman, she did get her children back. But it was only because her father's spouse was fed up with those kids. She demanded they be returned to Lynn and Norman.

As our conversation in the truck evolved, it came to light that this communal raising of children, particularly giving kids away, was not always done to suit the needs of the parents. There was a similar custom of giving your children voluntarily to a family without child, whether from death or infertility.

Lynn added another personal story, "We almost gave Jeremy to a white family. We had been friends for a long time when they lost their son in a car accident. He and Jeremy were best friends at Hardin High. Jeremy was happy to do it. But we didn't know how the white couple would take the offer. They'd lived around Crow, they knew the custom. But it wasn't their custom. We were afraid we'd offend them, insult them somehow."

I agreed, "They might think you're saying their son is replaceable." I added a personal experience of my own, "My two best friends from high school also died in a car accident. One of them, his Mom didn't have any other kids, he was everything she had. I never replaced him, but I have played a special role in her life. More than I ever would have before."

As I finished my sentence, Norman brought the car to a halt. He leaned over and reached under my passenger seat. He pulled out a big set of binoculars. As he raised them to his eyes he said, "That must be some boys comin' back from pasture. I wonder if they got a buffalo." As the distant convoy approached us, Lynn shouted from the back, "Oh, hey, that's my brothers, Jay and Dee."

Here we were in the middle of nowhere and we come across more of Lynn's family! And not exactly distant relatives either. Lynn explained that Jay and Dee's mother was her father's first cousin. They were raised, however, as brothers and sister. The bifurcations within Crow family structure were dizzying.

They had killed a buffalo and were quite proud of the evidence sprawled out in the bed of their truck. The internal organs were gutted, but the beast was otherwise intact. Bullets killed that Buffalo, but the pride of these Crow hunters was as if they'd been riding through the pasture atop white stallions pulling feathered arrows from sheaths strapped to their backs, firing off each arrow between high-pitched battle-cries.

In their hey-day, buffalo roamed the western North American plains by the millions. Crow life, along with life for most all the Plains Indians, was centered on hunting down these beasts. They were used for food, shelter, and clothing. Their existence was central to Crow life, both physically and spiritually.

When the white man showed up, he brought many gifts for the Native American, including a revolutionary new weapon, the gun. With the efficiency of bullets came total annihilation of the buffalo. As miles and miles of buffalo carcasses decomposed along the western plains, so did the life of the Crow.

What I saw in these modern hunters, riding around in pick-up trucks and hunting buffalo in confined space, was the shadow of a heroic past. Still, there was something in the spirit of these people that I surely did not have, a connection with land and animal that middle-class suburbia did not impart to me. The Crow spirit I observed was clearly alive, if not well.

Norman yelled over the corpse of the buffalo, "Hey Brian, you know what we Crow call a vegetarian?" He eyed the others knowingly, telling them without words not to rush the punch line.

"No, what do you Crow call him?" I replied, flashing a knowing glance that I was ready for his joke.

"A vegetarian is a poor hunter!" At this, the manly camaraderie poured out over the carcass between us. I could hear Lynn behind me throw out her standard, "Awe, shoot." She'd heard that joke before. She was laughing at these overtly masculine attempts at bonding.

"What does buffalo taste like anyways?" I asked.

Norman responded quickly, "Oh, its good stuff, but even the gravy is tough to chew!"

More laughter arose from the gallery as we climbed back into our trucks and parted company. The hunters went on to cook up their kill. We headed to cook up our plastic wrapped hotdogs.

We twisted down to the floor of the canyon known as Black Canyon. The surrounding mountains were rocky and covered with pine trees. We drove along a trickling stream until we came upon the Black Canyon Youth Camp. This abandoned summer camp provided an open space for us to park and set up our day camp.

Norman and I unloaded the firewood and prepared to chop them into smaller pieces. As we stacked logs on the ground, Norman put his hand on my shoulder and whispered in my ear, "Come here, I want to show you something."

We walked upstream from the campsite passing through some thick brush. We came upon a small clearing inhabited by an odd tent. It was shaped like a dome that had been flattened a bit. To enter, one needed to crawl. The shell material was a thick white canvas.

"This is a Sweat." Norman said. He described to me this traditional practice of the Crow Indians. It is an ad-hoc sauna that serves a spiritual function of cleansing the body. It is done with others of the same sex and in total nudity! Both men and women can participate but never at the same time. In any case, men always go in first, then wash up and eat while the women enter.

Chokecherry branches are used to construct the frame of the Sweat. Any canvas or hide is used to drape the branches, thus forming the Sweat Lodge. A fire is made just outside the Lodge with heated rocks. These hot rocks are placed in a pit inside the Lodge positioned on the right side. The patrons of the sweat disrobe completely and enter through the narrow entrance flap, which always faces east where the sun rises. Everyone takes their place around the left side of the Lodge.

A sacred line is formed from the fire outside to the entryway of the Lodge. No one can traverse this line except for the designated laborer. Breaking that line inappropriately draws sharp rebukes. Each person's role in the sweat is doled out by a senior person in the group.

Nowadays Sweats are done for different reasons. Many Crow do them as part of their daily routine. These folks are known as Sweat Hogs. You might hear them around town inquiring with the colloquial phrase, "Are you gonna build fire tonight?" Or they might skip the formalities and stop by a random Sweat without any invitation whatsoever.

Norman walked me over, pulling the front flap back to peer inside. I could barely make out a circle of grey ash on the ground to the right.

"Are we gonna do a Sweat today?" I asked.

"No way, man." He replied with that Mexican twang. "I don't do 'em anymore. I burned my ears last time and haven't done it since. So would you!"

Norman put his arm on my shoulder and pulled me away. We walked back to the campsite and found the girls cooking a pot of Chili. Lynn had a dual-burner Coleman travel stove sitting on the bed of the truck. They gave us a hard time for leaving our manly duties, namely building a fire.

Building a fire is #8 on the LOTIL. I was in a permanent state of readiness when it came to performing this task. It reinforced a base level of manhood in my psyche. With Shelley, I usually reminded her to throw out remarks like, "Wow, that's a *big* fire you built" and "How did you cut those big, heavy logs?"

Swinging the axe down against the logs, I barely missed my right thumb and my entire left foot on two separate occasions and I remembered why I didn't build more fires. Norman wrested the axe from my hands as his individual effort in accident prevention.

By and by, the fire was built, the grill was laid out and the dogs were cooking. We also grilled Bratwurst that I had picked up at the IGA in Lodge Grass. This was my specialty. I prepared them in the manner of any self-respecting Argentinean: before the Brat finished grilling, I filleted it open, cooking the open-face toward the fire. This charred the inside bringing all flavor from the inside out. It was eaten on a buttered piece of bread also charred open-faced on the grill.

I learned this while spending a college semester abroad in Buenos Aires, Argentina. There, it was called *choripán*. Vendors sold it from small mobile grills found on street corners throughout the city. My favorite was from a grill at the entrance of the Estacion Retiro, across from Plaza San Martin in downtown Buenos Aires.

Over Lynn's chili and the open-faced Bratwurst, the four of us talked about traveling. Lynn and Norman liked to travel, but lack of funds kept them close to home. They made it to Hawaii for their honeymoon, but they drank away most of those memories in the process.

Alcohol was another gift from the white man, first arriving with pioneer fur traders. In a culture of degradation and unemployment, alcohol was a drug too powerful to avoid. Death from alcohol related disease is consistently higher amongst Native Americans than in the U.S. population as a whole. Lynn and Norman had once worked towards being a part of that statistic, but they were clean now.

"In Crow language," Norman said, "alcohol is translated *bad water*. I've never seen one Crow who could handle his booze. They say it's in our genes."

Giving only hints, Norman's history with alcohol was particularly extensive. Life had been difficult for him, from his family situation to his own personal addictions. His unpretentious attitude proved he had come out of it.

Pretentiousness developed in those who had forgotten the lower depths from which they came, like they'd always existed in their present station. Norman had not forgotten. It was indeed very near to him. His humility towards God and other people was honorable.

We talked about other things, like Crow perceptions of homosexuals. Traditional Crow beliefs taught that a man had the spirit of a man, while a woman had the spirit of a woman. A homosexual was doubly blessed, for they had the spirit of both woman and man. In any of my circles of friends, I had never heard of homosexuality referred to as 'doubly-blessed'. But my circle had never included Crow Indians.

Our time around the afternoon campfire flew by. As the sun set over the mountains behind us, we packed up and headed for home. The ride out was a bumpy backwoods path to the main road. Climbing up the mountainside, we opened into a plain that edged toward a plateau overlooking Black Canyon. Free roaming cattle meandered about. Even horses ran without borders or fences in sight. The plain was golden but growing dark from the setting sun.

"This is my uncle's land, but he doesn't stay up here." Norman said. "He lives near town."

"What does he do with it then?" I asked.

"Nothing," he said. "He rents it to a white man and lives off the rent money from this land and another couple acres a few miles from here. Half the land on the reservation is not owned by Crow anymore, and what's left is usually rented out to white people, like what my uncle does."

Norman taught me the gravity of this issue, not only with Crow, but on all Native American reservations. The issue was sovereignty over the land. Crow had jurisdiction over the reservation, but they were not free to do as they pleased. Norman's uncle may have been renting it to a white man, but it was not of his own volition.

"It's easier for the white people to work the land." He said. "They get good loans from the banks. A Crow shows up at the bank for a loan and he's wasting his time. He might get it, but the rates won't be anything like what the white people get. He's better off letting the land to a white man." He paused for a moment but he didn't look at me. He stared at the setting sun.

Then, as though bucking those heavy laden thoughts, Norman said, "We're terrible farmers anyways. The Crow have never been farmers, or even ranchers. We were warriors, hunters."

The Rabbit and the Sun Dance

I stepped outside the Pink House on my first Sunday on the reservation. I knew there were a few churches scattered around the central plaza and I hoped to see how converted Indians transitioned from a pagan, animistic religion to Christianity. The morning air was crisp and cool, a harbinger of cold winter days ahead. I was overjoyed to hear the crunch of fallen leaves under my feet, #2 on the LOTIL.

I strolled down the street aiming each step toward clumps of fallen red and yellow leaves. I raised my head abruptly when the fender of a black Honda Civic zoomed past my kneecaps like a Times Square taxi.

A split second later, a white rabbit dashed into the street. Neither car nor rabbit realized what happened until it was over. The black Civic came to a screeching halt and saw what white flash had caused his front left wheel to bump. It then continued to the corner, turned left and disappeared. The rabbit was not so fortunate.

He squirmed on the gravel near the curb. His hind legs were crushed, functionally detached from his body though still attached by skin. His body went into spasm. His back arched and his eyes shot upwards, as though looking for something behind him. He was searching with great intensity.

After a few seconds, his spasm relaxed. He struggled once more to reach the grass lawn a few feet away. Now he breathed fast, shallow breaths. This rabbit was in shock. It was not much different than what a human being experienced when they obliterated one of their major arteries. He needed emergent fluids, blood, and surgery. This rabbit was actively dying. In the hospital setting, we call this 'circling the drain'.

Again he contracted back, and then relaxed. He repeated this cycle a few more times before jerking rhythmically to the beat of his heart that worked so hard and in so much vain.

This rabbit had a minute or two of life. I think even he knew that. I squatted next to him, watching his eyes and body as each breath counted down the seconds he had left to live. He arched once more, but when he relaxed his breaths became very slow. Only a few seconds remained. I watched his eyes intently. I was transfixed by the transition he was making from life to death. Finally, there was expiration and stillness.

I thought back to the man I saw in New York on my first day in Internal Medicine. Standing there alone in that room with a lifeless body, I felt a profound loneliness. Here I was now, standing over a lifeless icon of Easter, ironically a holiday celebrating resurrection, with that same loneliness.

I couldn't leave him exposed in the street, so I picked him up by those crushed hind legs and placed him into a nearby field. The tall grass covered him like a blanket. I assumed nature would take its course from there.

I continued on towards the plaza where I found a small evangelical church at the back of a dead-end street off the main town square. I was early and met the pastor of the church. He was a white man who had come from a Navajo reservation in the southwest United States. I thought it curious that even here, as it was in the hospital, leadership was transplanted material.

Sunday school consisted of a round table discussion centered on whether it was appropriate to participate in the yearly Sun Dance Ceremony. This ceremony is the biggest communal religious celebration of the year for most of the North American Plains Indian tribes. It involves elaborate singing, dancing, and drumming. Dancers fast for four days from food and water in a quest for visions. The ceremony takes place around a central wooden pole with a buffalo head impaled on top. I saw one of these wooden structures, without the buffalo head of course, in the restricted reservation area with Lynn and Norman.

During the Sun Dance, some tribes perform acts of self-inflicted torture. They run a bone through a loose area of flesh on their chest and then tie it to a rope fastened to the top of the center pole and pull until the skin is ripped off. This act can take hours.

Tradition requires participation four times in a man's life, reflecting the four compass directions. Though banned by Christian missionaries, and even by the U.S. government for the better part of the twentieth century, it is still an important ceremony to the Crow people. It also remains a hot topic amongst Crow Christians.

There were two perspectives on the issue, one strict and one loose. The strict line stated that any participation was an affront to Christ himself. The loose view saw beauty in connecting to ancient Crow traditions. They argued for remaining culturally relevant to traditional Crow beliefs, if only to proselytize more effectively.

Many Crow Christians have been ostracized to some degree from their larger community, especially if they reject any of the ancient Pagan beliefs or practices. But today's Crow have only a weak hold on these ancient beliefs, creating a spiritual void that Christianity seems to fill. Plenty-Coups himself said, "I hope, if they cannot find and hold firmly to our old beliefs, that they will learn the religion the white man teaches and cling fast to it, because all men must have a religion, if they would live."

It is man's need to know God, even to be known by Him, to which Plenty Coups refers. I felt it in myself when my eyes welled up listening to the Subway Evangelist in New York City, and frankly it is why he stood there singing in the first place. The poverty of the basic human experience as an end unto itself is played out over and over in every society, in every era. I wondered if the rampant alcoholism and depression in the Crow people was only a physical reflection of this spiritual turmoil.

After the service, I walked out into the crisp Montana afternoon. I felt spiritually refreshed like I always do when leaving a Sunday morning service. Especially when traveling far from home. I find in those moments a transformative experience, a connection with something that I cannot see, but that seems to be with me everywhere I go.

The Last Supper

Our last weekend in Crow Agency, Lynn asked Melissa and me to have dinner at their house. This would be my last time to see Lynn and Norman. I especially wanted more time with Norman. There are a few people in this world I am drawn towards like a magnet. At every opportunity, I pull up a chair next to them and let their wisdom, comedy, and their life experience pour over me. Norman was such a person, and I could hardly get enough.

Lynn swung by the Pink House and we followed her out to Reno Creek, a town consisting of their house and maybe ten others. From Crow Agency, it was ten minutes east down Interstate-90, just past the Little Bighorn Battlefield. We pulled up to their home as the sun was setting over a wide Montana horizon.

Lynn and Norman's house was a small ranch style one-story. The front yard was pockmarked by old cars and a couple of very large dogs. It was a better living condition than most Crow. Many houses on the reservation, as in the neighborhoods surrounding the Pink House, were in disrepair. They were completely subsidized by the U.S. government. How much was paid for a home depended on income, but few paid anything at all.

The tribal Housing Authority handled the distribution of the federally funded homes. Any Crow could petition for one, but the waitlist was long. Tribal politics being what they were, having a family member on the Housing Board got your name higher on the list.

Lynn and Norman were not dependent on the government like so many Crow. Lynn had her job with the Indian Health

Services and Norman worked in a coal mine. The Sarpy Creek Coal Mine was located off the reservation, but much like the farmland, Crow Nation owned the mineral rights to the coal while an outside company operated the mine. They employed many Indians from Crow. For Lynn and Norman, the opportunity to be employed *and* live on the reservation was a distinguished honor.

Norman greeted us in the yard as their rambunctious dogs led us to the front door. Inside, we were confronted by an enormous television. It took up the entire back wall of the living room, disproportionate to the small space of their home. Clutter was everywhere because they were remodeling the kitchen, yet another action incomprehensible to most Crow.

On the walls hung old pictures from hunting trips and from past Crow Fair celebrations. Thousands descend on Crow Agency the third weekend of August every year to celebrate Crow Fair. Participants camp out in teepees, lending it the title of Teepee capital of the world. There are parades, powwows (dance competitions), horse races, and rodeos. It is the pride of every Crow Indian, as evidenced by the walls of the Morrison home.

One of the hanging pictures showed Lynn dressed in a white-beaded, navy blue dress sitting atop a horse. She saw me staring and answered the question before it left my mouth, "Aw, shoot, that's from my wedding. That's my wedding dress. That cloth is the old kind of wool cloth that used to be traded by the Indians." She ran her fingers over the picture.

"Those white beads are ivory Elk teeth." She continued. "Norman's family gave me gifts and then paraded me on horseback at Crow Fair."

The purpose of the parade was to allow the groom's brother to show off his new sister-in-law.

"They're still working on mine." Norman preempted. Apparently, the groom could also be paraded.

Lynn continued, "I rode around and my uncle followed me as a Crier. He yelled out in Crow who I was and who was parading me.

"All those gifts, those blankets and beads, are shown off. In the old days those were a sign of great wealth." Her words trailed her as she disappeared into the hallway. She re-emerged with a white box in her hands. She sat it down on the couch. Inside was the dress from the picture.

"You can feel it. See the Elk teeth? Isn't it pretty?" She asked.

It was indeed pretty. I thought back to Shelley's wedding dress. It was a white satin dress with beaded floral inlays on the waist and train. I couldn't fathom Shelley in ivory elk teeth, trailing a procession around Moss Bluff, Louisiana on a horse. We did get a wedding day picture sitting atop a Harley Davidson belonging to her neighbor, Billy Parker. There was a semblance there, but it was a stretch.

What a difference the details make. The Morrison's are married, live in a home, have hobbies and a basic work-a-day rhythm to their lives. On the surface, a description of my life at home is no different. It is the rites of passage in our lives that most distinguish us as people. Ceremonies give human cultures uniqueness by expressing a society's most profound beliefs and values, done publicly so that everyone takes ownership of them.

We sat around the kitchen table and Lynn served a simple meal of chicken soup and bread rolls. Lynn was a sweet host, but not in the southern sense of the word. She had too many edges to be prim and proper. Yet her earthy kindness and practical expressions of friendship I found greatly endearing.

Our table conversation centered on the Crow people, their history and their traditions. Norman expressed a more open frustration about the on-going battle the Crow were fighting with white people. There was no anger in Norman's voice, just venting. It was a rare opportunity to express to a white man his deep discouragement.

In my short month on the reservation, I caught glimpses of this tension through off-hand remarks in the hallways and nurses stations of the clinic. From the Treaty of Fort Laramie in 1868 to the present day class-action lawsuit Cobell vs. Norton, which pits about half a million Native Americans squarely against the U.S. Government, only a politician could deny the litany of broken treaties and promises between the two sides. And they did so quite effectively.

It was not in Norman's nature to blame others. His life had been a fight to succeed against external forces, from overcoming alcohol to working and leading a family at home. He spoke about problems within his own family and people.

"Look at our kids today, on the reservation." Norman said. "They want to be hip-hop stars. Look at my own kids. I have always told them, 'your ancestors were warriors.' But they don't hear any of it."

I sensed a drop of pain, even shame, when Norman spoke of the Crow mentality today. This stood in contrast to the pride that usually sparkled in his eyes when speaking about his people.

He was right about the obstinate attitude of the present generation. In the hospital, and around the reservation, I noticed ghetto styles of dress and attitude. We were a thousand miles from an inner-city, yet kids sported gangster rap t-shirts and thuggish do-rags on their heads. They cruised in their cars with music blaring and thumping, mouthing lyrics about urban street life. How could this message resonate under the expansive blue skies of Crow Agency, Montana?

"They don't care about our history, our traditions." Norman said. "What will they teach their kids?"

The attrition of passing down the Indian heritage really began with the arrival of the white man. Even Plenty Coups ended his days working in a shop, without the glory his forefathers knew at the end of their lives. The icon of a warrior on a horse was now replaced by a fat guy munching down a fry bread taco.

Would Norman's nostalgia for the old ways and traditions of the Crow survive the apathy of the present generation? Indifference is a shovel used to bury traditions and customs. As Norman lamented, it was being flagrantly wielded by his own children.

I had always felt disconnected from my own ancestors, not knowing who they were or where they were from. The bloodlines that led to one's existence grounded the human spirit. Perhaps my desire to wander and absorb foreign cultures reflects an un-anchored soul.

So, I too was heartbroken to see Crow culture swept away by winds of change. This was a greater tragedy than my own floating soul. I longed for something I never had, but these Crow would long for something once held close. Like a widow they would mourn, and even now the pangs had begun.

I didn't share these thoughts at the table. I think Norman just needed to be heard. After we finished our meal and conversation began to wane, Melissa and I said thanks for another wonderful chance to know them and to learn about their people.

As we searched for our coats, Lynn and Norman whispered near the hallway. Lynn disappeared into the darkness and, as earlier in the night, returned holding two white boxes in her hands.

She sat them on the coffee table. While the boxes stayed closed, Lynn and Norman did something I never imagined possible before arriving to Montana.

Lynn began, "We have told you guys about our tradition of adopting children. Well, Norman and I want to adopt you into our family. We want you to be our white children!" Lynn let out her infamous 'aw, shucks' chuckle.

Melissa's eyes gleamed and gave away the happiness hidden behind the cracked smile on her face. What my face looked like I cannot say, but warmth filled my body.

"Lynn, are you sure about this?" I asked. "What does this mean? Am I estranged from my own parents?"

"It means you're part of our family now, that's all. Whenever you come to Crow Agency, you have a family, a place to stay. If you come to Crow Fair, you'll have a place in our tee-pee."

There was some ceremony involved before we became officially adopted. Lynn pulled the tops off of both white boxes while Norman spoke, "These blankets are a gift to you, sealing you into our families."

Norman pulled out a blanket for me. The pattern was a geometric design of repetitious triangles and jagged lines. It was colored with shades of chili red, burnt orange and yellows, and green over a black background. These shades varied like shadows cast in a late afternoon sunset. It was beautiful.

"It's a Pendleton blanket, very expensive." Lynn added. "It's a very honored gift among us Indians. These were gifts we received for our wedding."

Melissa received a different blanket, sealing her as well in the family. We thanked them profusely, but it still seemed inadequate. I wanted them to know what an honor it was to be a part of their family. I wanted them to know Shelley. She would be excited to have new relations in Montana.

We discussed coming to Crow Fair in August. This broke with my usual tact of cutting cords firmly - I was taking a risk. What would happen when Crow Fair came and went without a return visit? My enthusiasm to be a part of the Morrison family overcame my fears of distant ties.

As we approached our car to leave, I had a final important thought, "Since I'm part Indian now, do I get an Indian name?"

"Absolutely," Lynn responded, "but that takes a special naming ceremony. We can't do that before you leave. We'll do it when you come back."

I knew right then that it wouldn't matter if I returned this summer or the next, or ten summers from now. I would return one day and receive my Indian name.

Kenya

Chasing dreams

My journey to Kenya began with five BGU classmates on an Ethiopian Airlines flight from Tel Aviv to Nairobi via Addis Ababa. For 20 minutes, the line of boarding passengers sat congested behind two men and an old lady arguing over seat assignments and fumbling with their luggage in the overhead bin. The steward in charge, his obsessive-compulsive tendencies overwhelmed by greater forces of chaos, threw up his hands and barked out orders.

"Take any available seat!" He yelled. "Disregard your seat assignment and sit down!" That's what we did, and that was the beginning of my trip to Africa.

As a young boy, my father let me hold the wheel of the car as we drove across the border of a state. I proclaimed thereafter that I drove all the way from Louisiana to Texas. I still love crossing the threshold of a new land, especially when it requires a passport and a plane ride. People chase dreams on a plane (while on a bus they're usually running from them), and my anticipation climbed with the altitude.

My initial reticence in leaving home now gave way to a surge of curiosity about what Kenya held in store. I knew from classmates in former years that I'd be thrown into situations of increased responsibility. My medical knowledge and ability to make decisions regarding the care of patients was going to be tested by fire.

I hoped I would gain proficiency in diseases less common in the U.S.: malaria, tuberculosis, and the endless sequela of HIV/AIDS. I was frightened at the prospect of it all. With some distance still between me and African soil, I welcomed the challenge with the bravado of a teenager setting off for college.

Nairobi, our first destination, was the most dangerous city in the world. It had recently overtaken Johannesburg, South Africa for that infamous title. I was warned that walking around Nairobi in the daytime I was likely to be robbed; walk around at night and it was guaranteed. Our group therefore did not spend a minute more in Nairobi than necessary. After landing, we headed straight for the Nairobi Backpackers Hostel on the outskirts of the city. After holing up for the night, we made our way to Eldoret, a day's drive west of the capital city.

The Valley

Kenya's modern history was molded by over 600 miles of train tracks. The political will of Imperial England and the backs of subjugated labor from India laid down rails from the shores of the Indian Ocean to Lake Victoria, from Mombasa to Kisumu. The building of this train brought foreign influences still present in Kenya today.

Eldoret, a town created from passage of that railway, lies on the western side of Kenya high atop the escarpment of the Great Rift Valley. This valley is a monstrous fifty- mile-wide depression running north to south from Israel to Mozambique. We lumbered through this depression in a large white van that was sent from Eldoret to fetch us in Nairobi.

The group treaded lightly in conversation, not wanting to test the waters of personality conflict too soon on the trip. With so much time on our hands, there was no pressure to learn everything about everybody immediately. I was particularly reserved because the group was a quiet one, while I am comparatively loud and opinionated. At times these traits entertained, but other times they annoyed, especially over two months in confined social space.

We pulled into our guesthouse in Eldoret that evening after 48 hours of traveling. The six of us all but fell out of the van.

Luggage had been stuffed in typical third world fashion, making the impossible happen with sheer grit and muscle. It tumbled out of the van after us.

Bewildered from fatigue, we soon realized nobody was there to greet us. More importantly, no one had keys to let us into our new home. We looked at each other and the front door, knowing that a locked door meant that our travels would continue. Shira, a classmate who was ever inclined to act rather than deliberate, walked to the door and turned the knob. Much cursing did ensue as our group repacked the van and drove to the modest Eldoret Country Club. Though not extravagant, it did have a golf course that brought me great comfort in Eldoret.

Corruption over Nyama Choma

The next day was Sunday. The Club was having their weekly poolside barbeque and I decided to partake. I sat my water bottle down on a veranda table near the pool filled with African children. They wore goggles and swim trunks and seemed comfortable in their surroundings. They were obviously of privilege.

When I returned from the grill with my plate of Nyama Choma (Kenyan style barbeque), a regal woman was sitting at my table. She hadn't noticed my water bottle. She was pretty, and her traditional African garb belied her forty plus years. A blue head- wrap sat high on her head, evoking a warm glow against her dark skin. There were no other seats, so I took up my water bottle and asked to join her for lunch.

"And what are you doing here in my country?" She inquired.

"I'm a fourth year medical student. My medical program has a relationship with Moi University. There are six of us here for two months, working in the hospital and in a rural clinic."

"We can always use your kind of help." She replied.

"I suppose that's true. And what do you do Miss..." I realized I hadn't caught her name.

"Adila. Adila Jomo." She replied. "Yes, well, I work for President Kibaki's government." Mwai Kibaki was sworn in as Kenya's third president in December 2002.

"I am part of the Kenyan Transportation Ministry." She continued. "That airport you flew into is under my purview, as are all of Kenya's airports."

"How did you get that job?" I asked. I was intrigued to be speaking with someone in the Kenyan government.

"To be honest with you," she replied, "at the end of the day I am a politician. I have worked to help Kibaki get where he is, and now I am here. I have run for office myself, but have not been successful."

"So Kibaki got you this job?" I asked. "Do you know him?"

"Of course I know him," she replied. "This job is a presidentially appointed position."

I couldn't help but ask her about government corruption. Kibaki was elected on an anti-corruption platform, though he had made few gains towards that promise since taking office.

"Well, you know that corruption has been a part of every Kenyan government." She began. "In fact, Kibaki was elected on a mandate to clean out the corruption. Unfortunately the problem is deep and requires time, but the masses are impatient. People need to give Kibaki time. It will take five years at least for the new government to root out the corruption. But, people do not want to wait that long. But that is what's needed, I assure you."

While having lunch, Adila received a call from the personal assistant to the President. The assistant needed a favor regarding a personal business deal at a Nairobi airport. Adila promised to take care of it. I did not inquire about the details, but she was clearly needed to ensure a leg up on the competition. In light of our previous conversation, I was surprised when no explanation came forth.

After lunch, Adila handed me her business card and personal cell phone number, "Should you ever have a problem at an airport in Kenya, call me." I did not flinch in my acceptance of her offer. Governmental connections are enticing even to me!

Later that afternoon we finally made it home to the guesthouse. Located on a corner plot of land adjacent to the hospital, it was now open but not because of our arrival. The beige stucco house actually doubled as a restaurant for hospital faculty. A number of patrons were finishing off their afternoon meals on the lawn.

I shared one of three guest bedrooms with Nizar, the only other male in the group. I was thankful to have one other guy to balance out the girls. Nizar was a Palestinian raised in the United States. He promised to show me his home town of Ramallah, a West Bank suburb of Jerusalem, when we returned to Israel from Kenya.

We found ourselves right next to the restaurant kitchen. The room was painted sky blue, with a line of grunge along the walls from knee-level down. Nizar was convinced someone had painstakingly urinated around the circumference of our room. I couldn't prove him wrong, so I tried not to think about it.

The House of Mamlin

The buildings of Moi Teaching and Referral Hospital (MTRH) were simple, gray bricks cemented together without thought to higher level aesthetics. Few buildings had more than a ground floor. The grounds, however, were full of beautiful flowers and grass and trees. In this respect the hospital was to be envied, even by western standards. Unfortunately, that envy did not pass the entranceway into the medical wards.

I walked to the nurses' station of my assigned Adult Medicine ward, where I would spend the next two weeks. From there I saw most of the ward. It was sectioned into six alcoves, three on each side of the median passageway. Each alcove had eight beds, four lined along each side. The beds were simple metal or wood frames with four skinny legs. Each had a thin mattress for the patient to lie on.

There was less privacy here than my hostel in Manhattan. People were everywhere. The blue uniforms were the nurses. They scurried about flipping charts and leaning over giant wheeled tables that served as the pharmacy. The white coats were residents and medical students. They congregated around a patient bed in the second bay. Everywhere else and all around, like an old-fashioned horror house, were miserable souls sitting on beds in tattered clothes. These were the patients.

Patients and nurses alike stared as I approached the group of white coats. My blonde hair and white face showed like a lightning bug's bottom. I kept my eyes forward, not wanting to acknowledge the stir created by my presence alone.

When I arrived at the bedside, I counted myself the 23rd person standing around the attending and a patient. It was a sea of white coats and dark black faces. As the crowd shifted upon my approach another white face emerged. It was the attending, Dr. Joe Mamlin.

Mamlin was a professor of Internal Medicine from Indiana University, but his North Carolina heritage rang clear in his speech. "If I had to bet the last of my lunch money on what this lady's got," he said, projecting in a loud voice that befit his tall frame, "I'd be hungry for a week."

Back in Indiana, Mamlin was a legend for building the University's indigent health care system. In Eldoret, he was no less revered for spearheading a collaborative program between Indiana University and Moi University. Faculty, residents, and medical students from Indiana University were shuttled in throughout the year. They even paid for Kenyan medical students to do clerkships in the United States. Their presence at the hospital and in the city was palpable.

As rounds continued, I realized Mamlin's reservoir of knowledge was as deep as any I had encountered. He was the resident encyclopedia of MTRH. Mamlin's ability to transmit this knowledge with good ole boy simplicity made for a theatrical performance. I longed for each new patient in order to watch Mamlin churn out his bedside poetry.

Mamlin used the old fashioned tools of medicine to make the diagnosis: his hands, eyes, and ears. I watched as he measured out heart borders by percussion with his fingers. He stuck his ear to a patient's belly and shook, listening for fluid. I had never witnessed these maneuvers before.

In the Western world, the art of physical exam had atrophied from lack of use. Heart borders were defined by chest X-ray, fluid in the abdomen by CT scan. But on this ward, financial depravity made resources and technology hypothetical only. For example, not one CT scan was done during my two month stay as the city's lone CT scanner was broken. Even the simplest instrument such as an otoscope, used to look inside the ear, was nowhere to be found. Therefore, mastery of the physical exam was requisite. In the hands of Mamlin, they were alive and well.

This was the kind of doctor I longed to be, the depth of knowledge I wanted to have, and the skill sets I wanted to work with. It was these Yodas of medicine like Dr. Mamlin, Dr. Roberts in Montana, even the Eye-in-the-sky running the St. Luke's code who modeled the endpoint I sought in medicine.

Our group of 20 doctors, nurses, and medical students visited every bedside on that floor. The sights that I witnessed have never left my mind's eye for two reasons: the conditions of the hospital, and the commonality of HIV/AIDS.

In that first morning of rounds, I lost count of the times I heard Mamlin interrupt the presenting intern with, "Which one?" He wanted clarification of which patient was being discussed as most beds at MTRH held two patients. The feet and knees rubbed all around the torso, neck, and even face of their bedmate. An AIDS patient lay with a TB patient, and so the AIDS patient became the TB patient, if he wasn't already. To a man, their placid looks stated plainly, 'I expect no better.'

HIV infection was a scourge on the Adult Medicine floor. Roughly two out of three patients had full blown AIDS or were HIV positive. It was an asterisk by most every name, an explanatory footnote to their stories. With the toll of human suffering so rampant, it wasn't clear to me how HIV would *not* destroy Kenya, or all of Africa for that matter, in another few decades.

The difference between one patient and another was only the infections and complications resulting from their weakened immune system. HIV's modus operandi is to kill your soldiers, then let its allies attack. Infections with Tuberculosis (often the most devastating forms), Pneumocystis carinii, Cryptococcus, fungal infections and a textbook worth of other bugs were rampant.   Complications from the virus itself included encephalopathy and dementia. I was left to wonder what people in Kenya got sick from before HIV.

As we arrived at the last bay of beds, my gaze was drawn by an open, garden level window. The curtain was fluttering in and out with no screen to hold it in. I could see arrays of flowers outside, blue and red buds on dark green stems. I couldn't see the sky but the sun shined down on those flowers unfiltered, so I knew it was clear blue. This view contrasted painfully with the scene on the ward, especially the patient, Daniel Mwanga, lying below the window.

Daniel appeared quite healthy except for one body part. His left leg sat out from under his blanket, and it was monstrous. From a distance I thought he had replaced his own leg with a thick, blackened wood log.

At first I thought of elephantiasis, a filarial worm that blocked the lymph drainage system. Those legs could swell up to five times their normal size. I learned this was not elephantiasis however because, once again, HIV was involved. Mamlin expounded on Daniel's case of Kaposi's sarcoma, a cancer closely linked with HIV infection.

Was Daniel's leg just large and swollen, it would be an anomaly and no more. But covering every inch of his leg were grotesquely oozing lesions of pustules and ulcers. His leg was one large open flesh wound. As we approached his bedside, I was able to see more clearly these discharging super-infected lesions. I was also able to smell them. It was the smell of rotting flesh.

I also realized why Daniel lay here by the open window. Swaths of flies swarmed his weeping leg. He waved them away half-heartedly, his efforts no match for flies attacking necrotic flesh. It was a ghoulish sight that has become my quintessential image of medicine in third world Africa.

Lenai

In general, Kenyan people are as pleasant as the Eldoret weather. The staff at the guesthouse, the faculty at the hospital, and the medical students took extraordinary pride in welcoming all of us to their country. They did not withhold their smiles, which seemed bigger and brighter than any I had ever seen.

Of the Kenyan friends who welcomed us to Eldoret, none went to greater lengths than Joseph Lenai. I met Lenai at the guesthouse after our first day in the hospital. He carried a slender 6'4" frame, and like most Kenyans was mild mannered and soft spoken. He offered to be our guide in Eldoret. Two days later he toured us around the town, pointing out all the places to shop, eat, and use the internet.

Repugnant exhaust spewed out from the local open air bus station, greeting us at the entry to downtown. Raw and unfiltered, it jolted my olfactory sense into reflexive pauses in breathing, reminding me that I was in the heart of the developing world.

The human scenery of downtown Eldoret was chaotic. Pedestrians moved about everywhere; in groups, in pairs, and by themselves. Like an ant farm, there was a mysterious combination of chaos and purpose. Vendors with neatly aligned rows of clothes, shoes, calculators, and fruit pulled the crowds through every side street. The entire downtown was a thick, dark pulsating mass.

Those not on foot rode bicycles, often with stacks of objects piled so high the rider was forced to get off and push, making the bicycle an oddly shaped wheelbarrow. Traditional wheelbarrows were also seen. Young men, even children, made sport of sprinting through the human traffic pushing tomatoes, lemons, or piles of construction rods.

Cars entered the mix as well, racing through streets in a left-handed traffic pattern, an artifact of British colonization, at full throttle. Near misses with passing cars and wheelbarrows became passé because with every step onto a busy street, my first glance was always in the wrong direction. I considered it a victory that I avoided arching on the pavement like the Montana rabbit.

Lenai held hands with me as we walked the streets of Eldoret. It was a common sign of friendship in Kenya. A warm rush of embarrassment filled my torso as we strolled Eldoret's busy streets hand-in-hand. I was grateful to be counted a friend, so I fought the urge to pull away.

Redirecting my thoughts I asked Lenai, "Are the people of Eldoret one tribe?"

"Oh, Brian," he said with a slight roll of the R. "There are many, many tribes in Kenya, even here in Eldoret. See that man over there? He is from the Luo tribe." Lenai pointed to a man with a large, strong jaw and arms so long they reached close to his knees. Seeing another man of similar build I inquired if he too was Luo.

"Yes, certainly." Lenai responded. "There are also Maasai here, and the Kalenjin. The men you see running in Eldoret, they are Kalenjin."

Kenya has produced some of the greatest marathon runners in the world. Uniformly they hail from the Kalenjin tribe around Eldoret. I saw these runners when driving on the outskirts of town. They ran on the sides of red dirt roads, their feet treading lightly on the ground, propelling their bodies forward with the grace of a deer. Their lungs breathed the oxygen-thin air of Eldoret's elevated atmosphere, a great advantage in marathon training.

"I used to have a very difficult time determining you white people," Lenai went on, "All your faces look the same." A wide grin flowed from Lenai as he said this. He knew that white people had a notoriously difficult time telling Africans apart.

We continued our tour enjoying the company of a newfound friend, uniting ourselves by the wild differences between us. I calmed down as we walked, shifting my mindset to this new culture. I also felt better after making my only major purchase of the day: a travel sized chess board. It was a great investment for my journey in Africa.

And in this corner…

As Lenai broke off from our group to go study, I was drawn to a large crowd and booming voices over a loudspeaker. I didn't understand the Swahili, but figured that a speech of this fervor could only germinate from one topic: religion. As in the New York City hostel, the buzz of religious discussion was unmistakable. I could do nothing else but go and listen.

Roped off like a giant boxing ring, the crowd formed a human chain four people thick around the debate arena. With 20 yards of grass between them, opposing teams of four debaters faced off. Each side had a bench and a microphone. To my left, dressed in long white tunics known as kanzu with matching kufi hats, were the Muslim debaters. To my right were the Christian debaters. They wore western style khaki slacks and button down shirts.

The oral culture of Africa was on display in this debate. Back and forth they went, both sides arguing with fierce passion. They understood the key to turning a crowd. At the moment I arrived, the Christian speaker was building his case, climbing a crescendo in both tone and pace. At the peak, letting the rhythm of his oratory carry higher and higher, his arms fiercely pounding the air, he hit his point and crashed. Silence. The crowd on his side needed only a moment to let the point soak in, and then they went wild! Clapping and falling all over each other, they roared in approval.

Never in all my life did I want to understand a foreign language so bad. Frustrated, I called out, "English? English?" A tall man turned and, in broken English, said they were debating whether or not Christ actually died. The Muslims said he ascended straight to heaven. The Christians argued he died and only later rose from the dead.

This question was of primary consequence to the heart of Christianity. If Christ never died, then he did not serve as atonement for sin, nor was there any salvation in him. He would be just a regular old prophet, which is what Islam required him to be. In living around Muslims for a portion of my life, I was already familiar with this argument.

Without his death, however, the Subway Evangelist preached in vain; he had no reason to think that his lusts and deceits were abolished in any way. He would have to continue every moment of every day seeking forgiveness and hoping for the best. Whereas the promise of Christ is that forgiveness is instant and everlasting. And that is what I saw in his eyes that day on the train. There was power there, a peace that rose above a ruined and pathetic life.

I see this truth over and over, that as an effect of mans' need to know and be known by God, he also needs to resolve his moral dilemma; he wants to know that, despite his shortcomings, everything will be alright one day. I have known it myself through the guilty conscience I have lugged around since my youth. As I stood there amidst the struggle of men seeking spiritual truth, a part of me was still grasping that forgiveness, and trying to live in it.

Besides the subject matter, the method of discourse also intrigued me. In other African countries, like Sudan and

Nigeria, Muslims and Christians were slaughtering each other. In Eldoret, they held open debate in the public square. Each side held a cordial respect for the other and listened to their point. They even laughed after losing a point, realizing their opponent had won the crowd.

I was enthralled though I did not understand a word. I kept waiting for tension to develop, for an offense to be made to one side or the other. But it never happened. I continued watching their body language, tone, and energy, but it remained a vibrant and peaceful discourse. I was there so long my classmates ran some more errands before coming back to pick me up.

Learning to Breathe

Morning was my favorite part of the day. Our rent included breakfast prepared by the restaurant staff. I am typically a cereal-only morning eater, but the spread we awoke to was a luxury perk of developing world living.

I usually started with a bowl of Weetabix, a bark-like cereal that was fiber incarnate. Staying regular while traveling could not be a higher priority for me. Then I moved on to the fruits like *ndizi* (banana) and *mananazi* (pineapple). Every other day pancakes showed up on the table, causing quite a row among us since they were always one short.

Nizar and I walked over to the hospital together after breakfast. I was ready for a long shift as my team would be admitting new patients until the next day. Nizar had bailed out of the medicine rotation to work with some visiting Egyptian surgeons. He spoke Arabic with them and they accepted him with open arms which didn't surprise me. Even without the Arabic, Nizar is a talented conversationalist, someone you'd like to sit next to in a bar.

Nizar went out with them at night as well, playing Snooker at the Eldoret Country Club. He was especially amused by the drunken surgeon, Omar. This man always smelled of alcohol, even in the operating theater. He was quite famous for the practice which he claimed calmed his nerves. Such is medicine in the third world.

The day was uneventful for me until sunset when a patient went berserk on the ward.

"Where are my *watoto*?" He cried, searching frantically for his children while wailing about and screaming into the faces of the other patients. The look in his eyes was distant. The world he was in was nowhere close to Eldoret.

Odder than the behavior of this clearly altered mental patient was the reaction of the staff and patients. A crowd gathered as a security guard wrestled the patient to the floor. Their muscles were tense in a way that only physical struggle produced. I was tense because the altercation was so unpredictable. The crowd stood by amused, even laughing, as the patient got a foot shoved onto the back of his neck while still ferociously resisting. The quiet returned after the patient was removed and the other patients went back to their cots.

Around 8:00pm, Kenneth, a Kenyan student at my level of education and experience, took me by the hand to see our new admission. A younger medical student waited at the bedside ready to present the patient.

"This patient is a 51 year old man," the medical student spoke, "with two weeks of cough and difficulty breathing."

I looked around, surprised that he began without the intern, as the intern was officially in charge of the patient. Then I realized he was presenting to me, just me.

I shifted my weight from one foot to the other. I began to sweat. A terrible ache drew up into my abdomen. 'They expect *me* to diagnose this patient!' I thought. 'They expect *me* to make him well again!' I wanted to run away. In Montana, my word stood on a healthy baby. Here I was dealing with a truly sick adult.

"The cough is dry," the medical student continued without mercy, "and occasionally comes up with blood."

Then I blanked out, mentally derailed by an aspect of the patient's story. This habit was borne of years of passive medical education. At the patient's bedside, I was always protected by the attending physician. My mind was free to think objectively on medical concepts, or drift into other realms altogether. I was in no way responsible for the patient before me.

My reality in Kenya had changed. I was white and western and in their eyes I was expected to know medicine. There was no qualifier to offer now, no way to deflect responsibility. Fear tolled like a church bell in my ears, turning my focus back to the on-going patient history, "...no change in his appetite, but a 10 kilogram weight loss over the last two months."

The student's lengthy presentation carried on, mentioning every detail down to, "patient lives in a hut with no windows, one kilometer from the nearest water source, has six chickens and a donkey." When the student concluded, he and Kenneth stared directly at me.

I recognized those faces. It was my face a thousand times before. They held peace and expectation that all would be well now that an authority knew the patient's story.

"Brian," Kenneth asked softly, "what do you think we should do about this patient?" His narrow mouth was tense, but his eyes danced with intrigue by the patient's presentation.

A surge drew up in me to answer, but I could not move one muscle in my mouth. My vocal cords were taut. I was paralyzed not by a lack of knowledge, but by a lack of confidence. I didn't trust myself. But I had to speak. Those eyes, which now included the patient's, were staring intensely at me, waiting for a response.

"Well, let's see." My throat loosened up. I stopped pacing. "We should get some blood work on him, check a CBC, see what his white count is. Sounds like a TB case, so let's get a sputum smear and culture, and a chest x-ray and we'll take it from there. And of course we need to check for ISS." The term

Immunosuppression, or ISS, was medical jargon at the hospital for HIV positive patients.

The words flowed out of me. Kenneth and I discussed the case in more depth. My mind functioned in a way I had never experienced. I was taking my first breaths into a world of overwhelming responsibility, transitioning from a strictly absorptive state, to an active phase of practicing medicine. The first breaths were suffocating, but I was starting to love the oxygen.

Wilson and the Naked Habari

Wei, originally from China and the elder of our group, once pointed out that in Kenya there was only morning, afternoon, and night. The days crawled by and each of us embraced the pace in different ways. Shira read books, flying through at least two per week. Wei contemplated life and the ways that it would change when she married her fiancé in a few months. Nizar hit Eldoret on the prowl and found a Kenyan girlfriend immediately, which given the prevalence of HIV and their short lapse of time to sexual activity, had us all quite worried.

As for me, I played golf. It's a tradition in my family, even if I play the game poorly. My Grandfather was a golf pro in Baton Rouge. He played even after his leg was amputated as an old man, holding onto the cart with one hand and swinging with the other.

I went to the Indiana University compound, a gated haven of American lifestyle within Eldoret, and borrowed a set of clubs stashed away by an anesthesiologist who visited a few times a year. The walk from the guesthouse to the country club golf course was a mile or so and I did it with glee. I didn't worry about being tired since I didn't have to carry my clubs. Caddies only charged US$3.50 for 18 holes of labor.

I never had a caddy in my whole life. In the United States, they're reserved for professional players and the wealthy. But here I found myself obligated to obtain their services. In 18 holes, a caddy earned the better part of his month's wage. In not hiring him, he watched the sun set on another day of hunger.

Approaching the first tee I was greeted by a scene of 12 Kenyan men. Some lay on their sides, others sat gripping their knees. There was a great stirring amongst them as they jockeyed to carry my clubs. I found the caddy of the doctor whose clubs I now used. His name was Wilson.

Wilson was self-taught and had an impressive acumen for the game of golf. Wilson learned my distance so well that he fed my next club without consulting me. My golf game had never been so good.

Wilson reminded me of so many articulate and talented people I had met in the developing world whose gifts were stifled by the need to sustain life. There was no time for the extracurricular when your belly was empty. Fortunately for Wilson, he earned a meager living in a sport he enjoyed.

Exotic is the only word to describe Eldoret's golf course. Once again, I was caught in the pages of a National Geographic magazine, a Sports Edition. The course layout was simple with long straight fairways. The scenery and ambiance, however, was unrivaled.

Lined by lush forest on both sides, the fairway on hole number three undulated towards the green. In front of the hole, a stream ran across and into the woods. It was shallow, but the water was fast moving. Beyond the green was a long hill, brown with overturned dirt in preparation for planting. As I crossed the bridge arching over the stream, I came to a halt.

Upstream to my right, a teenage boy stood in the shallow water. He didn't notice me at first, but I sure noticed him. He was stark naked! His black skin glistened with dripping water, his feet the only body part under water. He was bent over towards me, rinsing his hands. This adolescent boy was in the middle of a bath! When he stood up, his glance met my stare.

"Habari!" He greeted me, waving his hand up high. There was no shame in that naked body of his.

"Nzuri sana." I responded with an awkward smile plastered on my face.

On the green, I stood over my ball, contemplating the scene around me. Besides the vibrant tropical colors and nakedness in the stream, I now heard the pressured beat of a distant drum. I froze enraptured by the stimuli I was receiving. It was so exotic, so foreign. I was in another world.

I didn't realize how long I had stood there until I noticed voices aimed at me. A security guard stood by a tree off the green. Beyond him, a group of children stood by the fence bordering the farmland. I smiled, gathered my concentration and proceeded to three-putt. I think the small crowd had hoped for a better showing.

The Sanitarium

The first weekend came upon us all very quickly, as did the first bouts of diarrhea. Our travel plans to go to a nearby national park were canceled as our guesthouse transformed into a sanitarium. Wei became Director General of this sick house, with Shira and I her first patients. At four o'clock in the morning, there was a convention at the toilet as vomiting and diarrhea consumed us.

Wei scurried about the house boiling tap water before running it through a purifier. Once she hydrated us, she rummaged through her belongings for a tiny canister of Tiger Baum. She was adamant that we rub this menthol-based cream over our temples, neck, stomach, and a discreet area below the patella of the knee. This would adequately treat our gastrointestinal illness, whatever microbial bug was to blame.

Wei preached the ways of Chinese Medicine saying, "Chinese say life has balance. Yin and yang. I believe this. You, Brian, have no balance."

She was right, but I didn't see how Tiger Baum medial to my patella tendon was going to restore universal balance to my life. More acutely, how would it stop this Escherichia coli from ravaging my intestines? But I did respect ancient Far East traditions, and anyways hope was fading fast. I permitted the remedy without protest.

Wei expounded on ancient Chinese philosophy while continuing to rub Tiger Baum on my knee, "Chinese say a person born with certain type of soul. Some have a young soul, some have an old soul. There are many kinds. You see it when they are young child. You see it by how they act. You know, that Mike Tyson, he has soul of animal. I see it in him. You cannot reason with him."

"What's Mike Tyson got to do with this?" I asked. "I think I was born with an old soul."

"Let me see your hands." She requested. She studied my palms, not speaking a word.

"Well! What do you see?" I asked. "Are you looking at my soul?"

"I not looking at your soul!" Wei replied. "I looking at your future."

I didn't believe Wei could read my future. But I had forgotten my nausea for a moment and could think of nothing better than to hear this revelation. Wei was reluctant to explain what she saw, so my interest in what she knew intensified. If I didn't believe she could see my future, I certainly didn't act like it.

Finally, she gave in. "Your money going to be very spread out," she said. "You will give away to a lot of different people. Also, you will have a career, but you will do something else. That thing will be greater than you career."

While I told myself this was well and ridiculous, I was silenced by thoughts of what my palms foretold.

My yin and yang feuded for four more tortuous days. I was so miserable I desired anything but to stay as I was. To get better would have been wonderful, to die an improvement.

Mamlin's wife, Sarah Ellen, kept a Sam's Club size bottle of Cipro at the Indiana University guesthouse. I hated taking medicine, but in the developing world Cipro 'cures what ails ya.' I gratefully accepted a three day supply, but what really saved me was something much simpler.

Oral Rehydration Therapy (ORT) revolutionized the treatment of cholera and the once pandemic death by dehydration wrought by diarrheal disease. It is little more than a liter solution of sugar, salt, and potassium, but it is the key to regaining health.

To my dismay, it was repugnant. Every sip reached the back of my throat and pounded my vagus nerve, eliciting a gag reflex. The result, however, was restoration of the balance I had been lacking.

By the time I fully recovered, my rotation through Adult Medicine was at a close. I was very disappointed by losing so much time on the wards. All I could do was cut my losses and know that more experience was waiting for me on the Pediatric ward. For now, our group was ready for some weekend travel. We aimed to see the most revered national park in Kenya, the Masai Mara Reserve.

The Mara

Our group descended the green tea fields of the Mau escarpment, a landscape easily mistaken for trim Berber carpet, in a specially outfitted van with retractable roof allowing all of us to stand up for an open-air view of the reserve. We were led by our driver and guide, Cyrus, and a travel-along cook named John.

In the valley below, at the cusp of the final leg to the Masai Mara Reserve, our van slowed to a stop. We gathered ourselves, pulling our bodies up and our headphones off. Before us remained six feet of pavement. Beyond that was uninhabitable African bush. The paving machine had obviously run out of asphalt, leaving the path to Kenya's most iconic national park to be traversed over nothing more than a vague dirt path.

A few hours later, and none the better for it, we sat at the park entrance. Cyrus, our driver, was out negotiating for us a resident discount. Women walked by our van adorned with pounds of necklaces and headbands. The Neon yellow, red, and orange beads radiated against their black skin. These were Maasai, the most well-known tribe in all of Kenya.

A few men drifted by and congregated near the back of our van. Their skinny torsos were engulfed by shawls of bright red patterned cloth. As I stared at them through the window of my van, I noticed that sunlight was beaming through their pierced earlobes, the openings of which hung down to their necks. A loitering youth worked his lobe with a small stick, while an older man hung his loops over the auricle of his ears.

We retreated to our campsite, discounted tickets in hand, ready to enter the park the next morning. On our way up the forested hillside, a herd of goats moved toward us in a wall of bleating flesh. Wei, ever the Chinese tourist, sensed the unique photo opportunity of a goat herd. From behind the windshield she clicked. The camera flashed.

From the morass of goats emerged a twelve year old Maasai boy. Draped in red and blue plaid cloth, his hair dyed red to match, he whipped his goats with a long, thin stick slightly shorter than himself and moved toward our van with resolve.

"You shall not pass without payment!" He yelled repeatedly in Swahili. I sat up in my seat thinking this pubescent boy was crazy if he thought we were going to pay him. Even as I gathered these thoughts, Wei handed him ten dollars worth of Kenya Shillings. She was clearly afraid and desired no more of a confrontation.

The Maasai, it turned out, had a clear understanding of the monetary value their unique culture held amongst the foreign visitor. Their fame in Kenya was centuries old by the time Europe's first slave traders and missionaries came exploring Conrad's heart of darkness. The Maasai warrior, known as Elmoran, was ferocious in battle, could run for a day without stopping, and could endure great pain. His accuracy with an eight foot spear was unparalleled, his willingness to use it, frightening.

Today, for a photograph, this Elmoran boy demanded payment on the spot. We saw this constantly in our stay at the Reserve. To visit their villages was a fee, to watch their traditional dances a fee, to stare too long at them a fee, even just standing near them could lead to a hand held out for payment. The Maasai still adorned himself with red cloth, dyed his hair with fat and red ochre, even made his earlobes into giant lassos, but was it still for a mystical belief, or for the month's wage he just received to stand in front of an odd machine that flashed? The transaction between Wei and the Elmoran was one step closer to the Maasai becoming a caricature of themselves.

Masai Mara Reserve, or simply the Mara, was an extension of the Serengeti in Tanzania. Defined by wide open savannahs of golden grass, with solitary flat topped trees pocking the landscape, its loneliness struck with the wind.

The desolation, however, was deceptive. Driving through the outstretched plains of grass was like staring at a forest floor. As you stare, ants and caterpillars and slugs slowly become visible. The empty plains of the Mara similarly awakened with leopards, gazelles, jackals, zebras, giraffes, and elephants.

The Mara seemed like an infinite, inverted zoo. We, the spectators, trapped in a safari van with a retractable roof, were the imprisoned ones; the animals were free to roam, free to act on their instincts, free to live out their natural way. I didn't enjoy the isolation and the relative immobility, but there was glory in watching the animal kingdom in its true form.

We followed a family of giraffes as they lumbered across the plain. We pondered the pressure required to push blood so many meters up that animal's neck, against so much gravity. It is said that a giraffe dies if they fall and can't get up; the loss of gravity without a compensatory decrease in arterial pressure bursts their brain's blood vessels.

Later, we watched silently as a solitary elephant appeared in the horizon. With unparalleled steadiness he approached our van, stood next to us for a moment, twirled clumps of long grass with his trunk and deposited the contents effortlessly into his ruminating mouth. Sizing us up, he passed along, disappearing as fast as he came. How a one ton animal appeared and disappeared so fast defied the senses. Certainly my New York patient, Big Momma, could not have moved with that animal's grace.

We made it to the slow moving stream that marks the Kenya-Tanzania border. We were greeted there by a monkey with sky blue balls climbing a nearby tree. Cyrus laughed at our intense amusement at this anomaly. He refocused our attention to the murky, slow moving waters before us.

Hippos ruffled the waters with gaping yawns that could fit me with room to spare. While these hippos were monstrous, they were lazy animals, and generally no danger to humans. The exception came if you stood between them and the water. The results could be a trampling and a low probability of survival.

The Mara's animal kingdom fed our conversations back at the campground while John, our cook, prepared for us a veritable feast.

"Shall I serve to you the local food of the Maasai?" He asked as he brought a large pot into our mess tent. We asked him what that might be.

"It is simple really," he said, "a little blood is drained from the cow's neck and then I mix it with milk!"

Seeing our appetites disintegrate before his eyes, John allayed our concerns with a smile and a laugh. "Of course I will not serve you such food. I do not have a cow! But for the Maasai, it is true, this is a daily treat."

John's meal was excellent despite my appetite that never did fully return. Around the campfire John entertained us with more local knowledge and tales of his own life. While he told how he learned Japanese to work with tourists, I sat there realizing

I had been quick to judge John's abilities by his station in life. How many travel-along cooks are linguists on the side? This stereotyping, a habit reinforced in medicine, often failed to enlighten me about a person's true gifts. John was proof of that.

Conversation waned around the dying campfire as my classmates trickled off to bed. Shira had long retired to her tent reading a book. Nizar was in the tent of two Danish girls staying on our campgrounds, though he swears they talked into the night and nothing more.

In the end, I sat alone next to the orange, sizzling glow of dying embers. This was #4 on the LOTIL, and fell above the actual building of the fire. Celestial lights studded that night sky. It didn't take long to see a shooting star arc across the great expanse above.

There was peace in that place and in that moment that I had longed for. Away from home, my wife, my people, traveling in a country where I didn't really belong but that had allowed my presence briefly. Those embers and stars were a dynamic portrait well-known to me. I was strengthened by their familiarity.

Sticker Apathy

Back in Eldoret, I entered a new phase of my African medical experience: Pediatrics. Medical school professors made it clear that Pediatrics is not Internal Medicine on little people. Everything acts and reacts differently in their little bodies. Their cells are young and full of hope, but still inexperienced in their work on this earth.

I was guided by two interns covering the Pediatric floor, Drs. Kwaro and Nakitare. Kwaro was a gentle fellow who wore a broad flashing smile at all times. He cocked his face at an oblique angle, hardly noticeable to the human eye. It bestowed on him an air of innocence and made him imminently approachable. Only when listening to a patient presentation did his face hold the contemplative stillness of a physician.

Nakitare was a young lady who matched Kwaro's affinity for smiling. I watched her being overwhelmed by one child's mysterious cough while simultaneously drawing up the chemotherapy regimen for another patient. Nonetheless, she needed only to make eye contact with me or Kwaro for a smile to surface. It stood at the ready, like Lynn's laugh in Montana, drawing up from the sides as though her nasal creases had the sole responsibility for raising her lips.

By day two, Pediatric rounds had become my least favorite aspect of working at MTRH. Crowds were as large as those on the Adult Medicine ward. The Pediatric attendings spoke at a notch above a whisper. Their accent, of British/African disposition, their local slangs and euphemisms, and their low volume made for a colossal struggle to pay attention.

And so I took interest in other aspects of rounds, like the mother who sat before the attending physician and a group of twenty medical students with her right forefinger lodged deep within the anterior septum of her nostril. She dug and twisted her finger while paying close attention to the attending's impression of her son's sickness. The attending didn't flinch, nor did the other students. I was aghast. Not only was it disgusting, it seemed disrespectful.

In Kenya, however, the common nose pick was not offensive in the least. I noticed it being performed by everyone! Doctors did it while listening to patient presentations. Presenters did it while presenting. There were no limits to this practice.

The woman sitting kitty-corner to the nose-picker held on her lap a child named Peter Kombo. He was so emaciated his face was that of an old man's. I tried to brighten his sullen mood with colorful stickers, landing one onto his foot, another on the back of his hand. He only stared, showing no recognition that he'd even been engaged. What disease so paralyzes the indomitable spirit of a two year old?

There was a diagnosis I feared in Peter, so I asked him to open his mouth. Holding my breath, I shined my penlight and saw a soft palate and tongue coated with white plaques. My heart sank as this was most certainly the fungal infection Candida albicans, also known as thrush. In the United States, I would consider this a routine infection of little consequence. But thrush can also be a sign of HIV infection, in which case it only warns that a legion of other enemies, with names like Cytomegalovirus or Toxoplasma gondii, had already staked their claim on this body. It was a death sentence for Peter.

Moving to the next corridor, I was startled by a vision I saw in a mirror. My head jerked back and I recognized that the vision of whiteness in the mirror was in fact my own face. My countenance glowed neon compared to my expectation of what a mirror should show. I had been in Africa long enough to be surprised at the sight of white skin, even on myself.

Sukumawiki and the Invitation

Because it was such a short walk from the hospital, we took lunch at the guesthouse. The menu was a long list of unexciting local dishes such as ugali (a doughy block of ground maize akin to grits), rice, coleslaw, and french fries. These complemented their exotic listing of meats such as broiled chicken, fried tilapia, and beef.

Whether you ordered it or not, sukumawiki found its way onto your plate. This salty dish is little more than cooked spinach and is a staple of the Kenyan diet. The name itself meant *to push the week* since it helps the average Kenyan get through the week without going hungry.

Lenai was there eating lunch on one of the numerous fold-up tables on the back lawn. I joined him as he ate his way through a plate of sukumawiki and french fries.

After ordering, Lenai told me he was headed to the U.S. for six weeks on a Medicine elective. Every year the Indiana University program sends 15-20 Kenyan medical students to study in the U.S., all expenses paid. Lenai was going to Salt Lake City, Utah.

"Yours will be the only black skin you see for that whole six weeks." I said.

"Brian," he responded with a wide grin, "how will I tell them all apart?"

Lenai had a way of speaking deliberately when making a joke. Like Norman in Montana, he never laughed at his own jokes. He let it linger in a purposeful way, curling his front lip over his teeth.

I decided to articulate to Lenai some of the important cultural differences I had picked up around Eldoret.

"First and foremost Lenai, do not pick your nose in public. You can swipe at it, but don't dwell. People do this freely in Kenya, but you can't do that in the States."

I had Lenai's undivided attention now. His fork hovered over that salty morass of boiled spinach while his eyes stared at me. He sensed the gravity of this advice.

"And second," I continued, "don't hold hands with other men when you stroll down the street or through the mall, especially in Utah. They'll have you pinned as a gay black man! Neither of which are seen in those parts."

Lenai had barely traveled beyond the area between Eldoret and Nairobi. My mentor in Louisiana, Keith Mayeaux, once told me, "Not everybody's momma strains their gumbo for 'em." He meant that when people grew up their whole lives in one place, it was hard to imagine other ways of life. Yet Lenai carried surprising insight into what the greater world might have to offer, that it might be very different from the reality he knew.

My food arrived. The french fries came out as ugali and the chicken as tilapia. This was not surprising since a third of the dishes I ate at the guesthouse restaurant contained food I had not ordered. Towards the latter days I resigned myself of the discrepancies and ate whatever I was given. The rhythm of African culture beat out the ingrained expectations of my Western upbringing.

Lenai then spoke up. "I want to invite you to know my family in Sipili." He said.

Now it was my fork that hung suspended in the air.

"I am traveling there in two weeks." He said. "I would like to take all of you. We will go to my parent's farm. I will show you what life is like in Kenya. And we will go visit my sister in Samburu land. You will never go there otherwise. It will be a great journey!"

Lenai offered a chance to know Kenyan culture from the inside and to lift another heavy veil of ignorance. His parents lived near Mt. Kenya. His sister lived in the north, a territory I was not previously keen on visiting. It is a desolate swath of land wild with bandits and, frankly, too hot to venture into. Who could say no to that?

"A great journey, indeed!" I replied.

The Code

I returned to the Pediatric ward to help out with the afternoon work. I knew from morning rounds that a few children needed lumbar punctures. I worked it out with Kwaro that I would perform these procedures. I had to be persistent about this since things often happened in hospitals without medical students' knowledge. We were an easily passed over commodity since we typically bore little responsibility.

A lumbar puncture is more commonly called a spinal tap. A needle is inserted into the spinal column to get a sample of cerebral spinal fluid (CSF). This fluid bathes the central nervous system, which includes the brain and the spinal cord. It can become infected, a disease known as meningitis. When caused by bacteria, it can be fatal. Any child with headache and neck stiffness must have this infection ruled out by lumbar puncture.

To perform the lumbar puncture at MTRH, we had the father hold his shirtless five-year old boy in a fetal position with his back towards us. Under Kwaro's instruction, I swabbed the insertion site clean with three swipes of spirit, the Kenyan term for alcohol. After securing the appropriate landmarks, I drove a run-of-the-mill intravenous (I.V.) stylet needle into the boy's back.

He jolted with such great force that three medical students had to help the father hold the boy down. The father laughed at this, which eased my distress. I drove the needle again until drops of off-white, watery CSF leaked out of the stylet. The drops were caught in a vile and sent to the microbiology lab.

I stuck around and worked with the interns, drawing blood and admitting new patients. I accompanied Kwaro and Nakitare to put an I.V. line into a kid with meningitis. The child was yet another notch on the belt of HIV/AIDS, this time Cryptococcus had taken advantage of the unlevel playing field and seeded his CSF. The child was so dehydrated, his veins were impossible to find. As I fished for a vein in his left arm, there was no response to the poking and prodding. This was beyond sticker-apathy.

"Is this child conscious?" I asked Kwaro.

"He has been semi-comatose for 24 hours now." He answered.

We evaluated his pulse. It was not palpable anywhere. Close inspection revealed stiffness to his tiny chest wall. This patient was not semi-comatose, he was dead!

Suddenly I found myself pressing my right palm into the child's chest. Brownish, blood tinged fluid poured out from his nose and mouth, synchronous with my compressions. My hand wrapped around from his sternum to his armpit. I gritted my teeth as I tried to squeeze life back into this body.

I pulled out my stethoscope to listen for heart or breath sounds. Kwaro took over chest compressions. Fluid continued to sputter from his nostrils.

"What do you hear Brian? Is he breathing?" Kwaro asked me. "Should we continue CPR?"

I was focused, my mind was clear. I understood the question he was really asking me, "If this isn't working, then how do we save this child's life, Dr. Neese?"

In our bedrooms and in dark corners of libraries, medical students learn the lines to recite in the human drama of medicine. We rehearse them in mock scenarios of no consequence. As understudies, we take the stage with trepidation, and everyone knows it is only a dress rehearsal.

In New York City, I was a fly on the wall during the patient code where I first saw death. Now, leaning over a small child in East Africa, it was my hands on the dying patient. My hands were feeling death. Ready or not, I finally took the stage.

"Clear his airway and keep bagging him. Keep trying for I.V. access." I said.

We kept running the code when one of the American residents, Dr. Jill Helphinstine, arrived. Jill was a Pediatrician fresh out of her residency at Indiana University. She was serving at MTRH for six months.

"What's going on?" She inquired. She picked up the boy's arm to palpate a radial pulse.

"He's not breathing, no heart rate. We haven't been able to get any access on him. Just giving CPR," I said.

"That's all we can do," Jill replied.

Another minute passed, though it dragged on like a hundred. Nakitare showed up with a syringe. She flicked the top of it with her finger, squirting a fine stream of excess fluid into the air.

"There is one more thing we can do...epinephrine." She stated. She did not break her gaze on the syringe.

She measured a space on the left side of the boy's chest. She drove the needle to the base of the syringe, injecting adrenaline directly into the heart. It was a scene straight out of *Pulp Fiction*. Sadly, we could not overcome the sepsis, the meningitis, or the other damage already done. We examined him once more and confirmed there were no heart sounds or spontaneous breathing. His pupils were fixed and dilated and not reactive to light. We declared him dead.

I wanted to reach out my hand and heal him. I almost felt that I could. Instead, I did what comes so naturally when a life passes from this one to the next. I prayed. Without any reason to think it would make a difference to this child, I feebly committed his soul to the Lord.

I wonder how long I stood there, staring at the child. In what was probably ten seconds, I saw everything he would have done, the events he would have influenced, the ripples his life force would have created in the world, and they all dissipated into a mist before my eyes. I stood at the threshold where my own limitations met with God's sovereign plan and the limits of the natural world. It was a painful place to be.

I stepped back from the bedside until I bumped into someone. Turning around, I found a woman sitting on a stool. Her face was buried in her hands. Quietly she sobbed into her yellow tattered, cotton blouse. I could barely hear her crying, yet no sound ever penetrated me more.

Sirens

Nizar and I headed downtown to check our email at a local internet cafe. We held dear this thin connection to Western civilization. We had tried every internet cafe in Eldoret. Most computers were suffocating, taking two minutes to load a page. Others had jammed keyboards. It was a hassle until we stumbled upon a small, hole-in-the-wall café without even a name.

Directions to our internet oasis went like this, "Go to the right of the main traffic circle, next to the corner hardware store by the woman selling lemons but just before the woman selling used clothes on the street. Enter past the little bakery and up the stairs, swing to the left, then through the sign-less door on the right, next to the dentist's office." When sharing this with expatriates, they usually paused to draw the mental map and then responded, "Oh yeah, that's the best place in Eldoret!"

It was dusk when we walked back, content with even mundane news from home. The walk towards the hospital, and our guesthouse, followed a steep incline. Most of the Tuk-Tuk's had to dismount their passengers and push their bikes up the hill.

The hospital was perched on level ground, but it hovered above the city casting the only nightlight Eldoret knew. We carried a flashlight because light or no light, the streets were always busy.

Nizar was in mid-sentence when I stopped cold in my tracks. He walked ten feet ahead before realizing I wasn't beside him anymore. We were passing a large church below the hospital called the Africa Inland Church (AIC).

Music emanated from a small building on the church grounds adjacent to the main sanctuary. I heard singing like I had never heard before. I froze in place, entranced by soulful, angelic sounds. Like sirens from Homer's Odyssey they pulled me in.

I broke off from Nizar and followed a steady stream of young adults. They stepped through a wrought iron gate and filtered into the building. I stepped through as well and immediately became apprehensive. I was so white and there was no hiding it. I was about to step into a room full of strangers and shine like a fluorescent bulb.

Fortunately the group was in prayer. I scurried to the back and took my place on the craggy wooden bench that served as a pew. The room was rather small, with soft pastel colors on the wall and a low roof, but it was filled with young adult Kenyans. I watched closely to gauge what purpose this service held. Everyone was praying at once, softly praising God to themselves. Though independent in their praise, the group was undulating together as one body. The crowd quieted down. Even this was done in unison without any particular leadership.

Someone finally stood up and addressed the crowd. He was a young man, with eyes blazing white against the background of his jet black skin. His teeth were equally white, flawed only by a small space between his front teeth. He spoke softly, but his words came strong.

"Brothers and sisters, welcome to the house of the Lord!" His eyes danced as he spoke. "Tonight is a chance to worship the one who made you, who stitched you together in your mother's womb. Let us praise him as one voice."

I couldn't help but remember the Subway Evangelist. They both spoke with a vivaciousness that belied their humble appearance, and with similar African accents. It was something of a déjà-vu experience, as on the subway I also was part of an audience swaying by a force out of my control, enraptured by a speaker who emanated passion and love.

I found out from a student next to me this was a Christian Student Fellowship connected to Moi University. The preacher was only a student leader. After giving a short sermon on the need to stay committed to the Gospel of Christ, the speaker led the group in more singing, like the music that first drew me in. Again the group swayed in perfect rhythm, their bodies flowing without pause or stutter. I swayed too, but it was difficult to match the internal rhythms around me. For whatever reason, I was not designed to exercise such freedom of motion. It was no matter though. My heart was melted by the music and even the lyrics, whose Swahili tongue I did not understand.

I became aware how spiritually dry and thirsty I had been. And now, a summer rain was falling over me; I had only to stick out my tongue and drink. I was dealing with loneliness from missing my wife and home, and with the emotional trials medicine brought at the hospital. My hands had held death in their grip, amongst other sorrows found on those hospital floors, and it was certainly taking a toll on my well being. The fellowship rejuvenated my spirit to carry on, and to love, and to continue the work that brought me to Kenya.

Sipili Shamba

The weekend arrived for us to visit Lenai's family in Sipili, a small agrarian town in Laikipia District in the center of Kenya. The highway out of Eldoret took us down into the Rift Valley, crossing back and forth over the Equator. We found this to be quite novel, as if the equator only existed in Kenya.

At the back end of this four hour trek, our vintage 1970's Peugeot hatchback fought through pot-holed highways or worse to arrive at the squares of farms that made up Sipili and the shamba of Lenai's family.

After visiting the town chief to let him know muzungus (Swahili slang for White person) were afoot, we came to the dirt path leading to Lenai's shamba. Three women greeted us, including Lenai's mother, dancing and clapping their hands.

"Welcome, Welcome," they sang in the Kikuyu language, "Nawakinya kwa Lenai-ie, siti downi. *When you get to Lenai's place, you'll sit down.* They followed our car not letting up a beat. Pulling each of us out of our bench seat matatu wagon, they kept on singing.

When the singing stopped, communication became difficult. They spoke no English and we spoke neither Kikuyu, Turkana, nor Swahili. But smiles went a long way to show their welcoming hearts, and our thankfulness to them.

Each dwelling on the shamba was made of mud brick and wood slabs, with a roof of tin or thatch. I stepped into a nearby hut while the others talked around the car. A fire burned in the back corner, filling the small square room with black smoke. There was no chimney and no draft from the lone window. Piles of silver pots clustered in the corner, and an elderly woman sat on a low wooden bench near the fire, completely submerged in smoke.

I stepped out and ran into Lenai. He pointed to the nearby outhouse, offering the facility should I need it. He said the wooden structure there now was the second his family had built.

"The other one stood there," he said while pointing to an eight foot high banana tree. Wide green leaves hung low towards the fertile ground. "It lasted thirty years before we topped it off with dirt. We waited a year before planting that banana tree."

Lenai then walked me over to the animal pen where his father was standing.

"Brian," he said, "this is my father, Etilon."

Etilon was as tall as Lenai with big, calloused hands. His eyes, whose white sclera was stained yellow, appeared curious but not enough so to bridge the enormous divides of culture and language. He stood there in his tattered denim Kangol hat and Mickey Mouse t-shirt quietly smiling.

His eyes suddenly perked up and he walked over to the farm's resident donkey. He returned and stood proudly next to his beast of burden.

"He wants you to take a picture." Lenai said. I took the picture, but even then Etilon did not speak. He didn't even ask for a copy of the photo. He simply walked away. The difference between Lenai and his father seemed profound.

"You are a medical student in Eldoret." I said. "Your father has never left this farm. What in the world do you talk about with him?"

"What do you mean?" Lenai responded.

"What do you two have in common?" I asked. "Do you talk about farming?"

"Oh, Brian," he replied, "If I had any talent with a hoe my father would have never let me leave the shamba. When I was a young boy, he saw that I was useless to him here. He was not happy with me. He sent me to a Catholic boarding school."

"You would have never been a doctor then?" I asked.

"Never," he replied. "There are no guarantees in schooling, only in work."

My classmates started walking by with their bags in hand. Lenai's mother, Esther, was leading them to their quarters. Her skin shined and was pulled taut over the sharp curves of her nose and mouth. Her hands were every bit as thick and calloused as her husband's. And though she dressed in a woolen sweater and walked around barefoot, it was obvious that were she born to metropolitan roots, she would've been a woman of elegant beauty.

I joined the group and we were all ushered into a mud hut Lenai had built a few years prior. It was a large room sectioned into three by two walls. Without an inch of open space, the walls of the inner room were covered with magazine and newspaper cutouts. There was no rhyme or reason to them, from random advertisements to sports stars not even Lenai was familiar with.

Lenai worked frantically with his mother moving three hundred potatoes to the corner of one room and sweeping away a pile of ants in another. When the room was ready and our bags tucked away, we were led outside once again to see the small half-acre field where the family grew their sustenance crops.

Esther bent over at her hips, keeping her legs straight, and pulled with great force at a root in the ground. With a final heave she yanked the root free.

"This is cassava," she said through Lenai's translation. "I must cut out the core or it may kill you." She tapped at the center with a big knife. Lenai took the liberty to explain the core contained cyanide and could indeed be fatal if ingested.

Walking the perimeter of the shamba, we saw row after row of maize. Along with cassava, this was a staple food in the African diet. Beyond their crop field were a hundred more, and beyond that I saw the sun setting over the horizon. I think I only notice the sunset when I'm traveling. It is a sign that my body has calmed and my eyes are vigorously absorbing the world around me.

Upon returning, we waited in the center room of our hut for dinner. We read the wallpaper about discounts on tennis shoes in Nairobi from the year 2000. As the sun began to set, the women and girls brought forth from the smoky kitchen hut a traditional African meal. There was white rice, boiled chicken, cabbage salad, and roots of various origins, including the blessed cassava. There was mokimo, a mashed potato dish mixed with green peas, and of course ugali.

They also brought out beef stew, but I avoided this liquid dish. I took to heart the famous travel rule: boil it, peel it, cook it, or forget it. If I didn't watch any of those happen with my own eyes, I did forget about it. Soups presented as much gastrointestinal danger as drinking straight from the farm's cistern.

In any case, I chased the meal down with two tablets of Kalbeten, the Israeli form of Pepto-Bismol. I could not escape paying some price for the authenticity I was enjoying. The outhouse on the shamba was posh in that heel boards were arranged in relation to the target hole, ensuring one's center of gravity was appropriately placed while squatting. There could be worse situations than to have diarrhea with this quality of a hole in the ground.

There was no electricity and the sole lamp in the room was not very bright. Lenai's brother ran a mile down the road to fetch more oil for that lamp. In the growing darkness, we were all very content, especially Lenai.

When our paraffin was about to give way for good, Lenai leaned over to me and said, "I will show you where you will sleep."

I was surprised that I would not be sleeping in the sectioned hut. We walked over to his little brother's one room hut and he opened the door. The room was little more than four mud baked walls and a dirt floor. A writing table was pushed up against the wall, the only piece of furniture besides the bed.

"Thank you, Lenai," I said, "I know I will sleep very well tonight." Wishing me goodnight, he left me in the room alone.

I pulled up to the writing table to write a letter to Shelley. I felt a sense of purpose, as though not writing down my thoughts at that exact moment would be a great injustice to her. I wrote the following: *Shelley, Right now, I am in Africa. The light at my side is flame burning paraffin, the walls that insulate me are of sun-baked mud, the roof covering my head of tin sheets. I am on the shamba, and I am experiencing Africa; as true a version as a muzungu can know. I am as content as a wanderer could be.*

I folded the Air Mail paper and placed it into a hidden compartment in my JanSport backpack. Then I embarked on a wonderful night of dreams.

The Grace of God

The next morning we left the shamba waving to as many as had greeted us the day before. The dry heat made the dust kick high behind the wheels of our car.

"My father is sparing his favorite goat for your return," Lenai said as his family and friends faded from our view. "We will share in Nyama Choma, a homemade Kenyan barbecue at that poor goat's expense!"

Lenai's cousin, Agnes, lived in a town of fifty people along the way to Samburu land. We stopped to visit and Agnes sat us down in the living room of her tin shack property. Lenai mentioned that her business was working with cow hides. I didn't see any evidence of that vocation except for the flies that swarmed around us. There were flies on the wall, on the table, on the windows, on the couch, on our hands, and on our faces. It seemed that invisible fecal matter coated every inch of that living room.

Agnes brought us cokes while her nine year old son tried to play a cassette tape of early Michael Jackson hits on a broken down boom box. It was a gracious attempt at ambiance, trying to make her foreign guests feel at home. We hastily signaled to Lenai and made our exit.

We next came to Rumuruti, the small municipal hub between us and the hinterland of Samburu District, the home of Lenai's beloved older sister and the goal of our weekend journey. We took a short break for lunch and I was able to find a mailbox for Shelley's letter. Mailing a letter is #11 on the LOTIL because I always experience time travel in the process. The letter falls away and its actions on the reader occur, from my perspective, at that very moment. That Shelley would not experience that reality for three more weeks was arbitrary.

From Rumuruti, we made it ten miles up the road north before our matatu finally gave out. The engine was dead and there was no saving this car by any of us, including our driver.

Gathering curiously around our matatu, Maasai warriors showed up out of the woodwork. Wearing brilliant red shawls and beaded bracelets of every color in the rainbow, they stood on one leg while leaning on their long staffs. We stared at them, they stared at us, and all of us stared at the hunk of white and yellow metal that had stranded us there. More locals showed up to examine, contemplate, and pull on this or that rubber cord. They made gesticulations towards our driver, and one-by-one they walked away.

Shira and I sat on rocks on the roadside contemplating how many Maasai warriors it took to fix a 1979 Peugeot. About that time, the bill arrived for the authentic Kenyan food I had consumed at Lenai's shamba. My abdomen cramped in an all too familiar fashion. With a trusty roll of toilet paper flattened and stuffed in my pocket, I walked the dirt road looking for private space. I was ecstatic when I came upon an outhouse a quarter mile down the road on a small, shrubby shamba.

Flies flew in and out of that hole in the ground. But after Agnes' living room, I hardly noticed them. I was becoming endeared to the common squatter toilet. The trick was balance. Unlike Lenai's posh elevated planks, this outhouse required grabbing hold of a metal piece of framing. Wei told me later that she was raised on such squatter toilets. She said that people in rural China swear by them for cleanliness to the user. Once again, who was I to argue the ancient ways of the Far East?

Upon my return, the local Maasai warriors and Turkana elders let it be known that a muzungu lived on top of the hill at whose base we were stranded. Hope was infused into our group as we eagerly hiked up the winding path of brush to the top of this small hill.

We came to the barbed wire gate of the compound and were greeted by a wooden sign that read, *Enter at your own risk.* An old dog sauntered towards us without even barking. He didn't care much about anything, let alone our presence at the gate.

A slim man with thick brown rimmed glasses appeared before us. His white t-shirt and brown high rise shorts went well with his dark socks and tall hiking boots. Against all of this was white skin well-tanned by the African sun.

"Hello, sir," I said, "I guess you can tell we're a little lost."

"My name's John," he replied as he unlatched the gate. He stepped out to us and offered his hand. "John Perrett."

In a way peculiar to being stuck in the African bush, we did not immediately discuss what our group of foreigners was doing at John's gate in the middle of nowhere.

"Where are you from?" I asked.

"Kenya," he replied.

I had obviously implied, 'You're white and western, so how did you end up on this hilltop in Kenya?' Yet no explanation was offered.

John did offer to descend the hill and evaluate our stranded vehicle. He spoke with our driver in Swahili. To my surprise, there was no hint of an accent. He soon diagnosed an amenable problem of electrical circuits. He also delivered the hard news that it required a trained and well supplied auto mechanic in Rumuruti. John then bid us adieu, "Let me know how I can help, should you have need for it."

We were no doubt in need of help. An hour and a half into this ordeal and we were firmly stuck in a non-proverbial rut. Should the sun set on us, we would really be stranded. Where would our car, or we for that matter, pass the night without being looted? Our most tangible hope in the form of John Perrett was now gone.

Lenai and I decided to hitchhike back to Rumuruti. We could acquire the necessary mechanical help and return with them to have our car fixed. But only two cars passed by over the next thirty minutes. They were matatus filled to overflowing and they barely gave us notice. Our hearts grew heavy as the sun moved steadily across the sky.

The next vehicle that came barreling down the dirt highway was a dark green truck with a canvas covered cab. Thirty meters away, I could see a white man at the wheel and a white woman in the passenger's seat. This was no matatu.

Forming a prayer tent with my hands, I begged for mercy from a fellow white man. The vehicle blew passed us but we saw the red brake lights kick on as the truck pulled to a stop. Dust floated over the truck like a great fog and filled our mouths and nostrils as we ran towards the driver side door. The driver motioned to hop into the cab and without question I climbed in with the two muzungus. Lenai climbed into the back where a number of Africans were riding along.

"Thank you! Thank you for stopping!" I exclaimed.

"My name's Barney Gaston, this is Suzie Armstrong." He replied. "It's no problem at all."

"Where are you from?" Suzie asked me. Again it struck me as odd that my being stranded in the desolate plains of rural Africa did not demand an explanation.

"I'm from Louisiana," I replied. A spark of recognition emerged from Suzie's face.

"I was living in Austin, Texas before I came to Africa!" she exclaimed. "I grew up in Michigan, but I need heat. I loved it in Austin. It was hard to leave but I came to work with refugees in the Sudan."

My heart was leaping in my chest. We talked about Texas barbeque and Stevie Ray Vaughan and other novelties of life in the Deep South. In the cab of that vehicle I was transported home for a moment.

"And where are you from, Barney?" I asked. I didn't want to ignore the person responsible for this merciful ride.

"Kenya," he replied.

I waited for an explanation, though I was quickly acclimating to the White Kenyan's sense that he was not peculiar in the least. Suzie's warmth, however, emboldened me to push for more.

"There is a man that lives on top of the hill where you picked me up..." I began.

"John and Amanda Perrett," he interjected. "Yes, of course."

"He told me he was from Kenya too. But pardon me for pointing out that ya'll don't look like the Maasai warriors standing around my broken down car."

"I see," he responded. "Well, my grandfather was the British Governor of Kenya in the days of Colonial rule. My family has never left. John's parents were English as well. Kenya is our home. It is our children's home."

The ten miles to Rumuruti flew by in seconds for me. Barney and Suzie dropped us off wishing us well. It was an anticlimactic end to a fortuitous relationship, but a trek through the developing world demanded such good fortune to balance out the inherent misfortune in traveling there. There was no need to belabor that fact with ceremony.

I followed Lenai as he negotiated a deal with two auto mechanics. My presence was an asset to Lenai, since white-man-stranded-on-desolate-highway was like winning the lottery for a mechanic in Rumuruti. He knew I had money and could extort me for it. I argued on principle, but in the end I paid. It still cost less than taking my wife out to eat in Boston.

With our mechanics in tow, we walked to the main street searching for a ride back. We were negotiating a deal with a local taxi driver when a huge bus came barreling through town. *The Grace of God* was written in giant red letters across the front windshield. It was a public matatu, not a religious vehicle at all, and it was headed towards our stranded vehicle.

As we boarded and began down the road, I asked Lenai, "Why does every matatu in Kenya have something religious written across their windshield."

"We are very superstitious in Kenya," he replied. "They hope to keep bad things from happening." Lenai threw his hand open towards me and asked, "Do you not believe in such things?"

"I never travel without a Bible in my backpack," I answered. "So, yeah, I guess I do."

The bus navigated the sharp bends of dirt road and the open landscape of the African bush. The driver occasionally pressed his horn to startle away goats wandering in the road. The horn sounded the high pitched squeal of a saxophone.

"Brian," Lenai began, speaking my name with that delicate roll of the R, "I will tell you something that very few people know about me. My close friends I do not tell this to."

Even with the bumpy road and the dust that kicked up around the wheels and wafted into my eyes, I had no problem focusing on Lenai's next words.

"I had a dream when I was young, maybe I was nine years old." He began. "I was speaking to a congregation of my countrymen. It was a very, very large gathering. It was all of my people, Kikuyu, Turkanas, Luo, yes the Maasai as well. All were present, and all were listening to me speak. I was speaking very powerfully to them. They were looking to me for leadership. I was moving the crowd with my words. It was a powerful dream for me. The next morning I spoke with my mom and I did not mention my dream to her, but she surprised me. She told me of a dream she had that same night. She was in a large crowd of people, and she was crying because the speaker at this gathering was so powerful. The speaker was me, her son, Joseph Lenai."

Lenai paused, staring at me but lost in his own recollection. He continued, "She told me this was a sign that I will be a great man one day. I will be a leader of my people. She told me not to worry anymore about this dream; it was our secret. Ever since then I have known that I will do great things."

Lenai's past, and his present, suddenly made complete sense to me. He struggled from a life without social privilege and loosed himself from agrarian seclusion to become a physician. Those achievements would be impossible without a profound sense of purpose. In Lenai, it was all-consuming. It was the force squeezing blood through his veins.

Our moment of kinship dissipated quickly when a ruckus began. Our bus was making an official stop in a place with no signs of human life. Only a dry creek bed ran behind us, and of course dusty brush as far as the eye could see. Shouts exploded outside the bus. I stood up with Lenai and saw our bus driver attacking an adolescent boy!

The boy squirmed from the clutches of that middle-aged man. Every piece of his clothing was torn off, except his shorts. A shouting match ensued. A friend tried to calm the boy, but his face was caged in rage.

Suddenly, he picked up a rock, a large one, and hurled it at the bus driver. He missed by a foot, no more. He threw another, barely missing again.

My eyes were plastered to the back window of the bus. Lenai came into my view. He was out there trying to make peace. A rush of fear passed over me. How far would this escalate? What were the limits of crime and punishment and rage in the remote plains of Africa? I felt the isolation of my geographic location.

The boy threw another rock, which again sailed wide right. This gave the bus driver and his assistant the courage to give chase after the boy. He was speedier than they, and he was fearful. He vanished like a rabbit into the brush.

The rage and the shouts calmed down and everyone returned to the bus. Lenai's emotions were still engaged in the altercation. He did not speak until the bus started on its way.

"The boy stole milk from that woman," he said, pointing to a woman with a child sitting across and behind our seat. "It was milk for her children. This is sad, Brian, so sad. I am sorry you had to see this. Some people..." He didn't finish his sentence.

We arrived at our stranded location and took our mechanics to the still open hood of our Peugeot. A roadside trading post that wasn't open before was now bustling with life. Wei and Shira had the chess board laid out on the dirt beneath the shade of a small tree. A crowd of curious onlookers gathered around them.

I noticed Lenai had engaged two elder men standing close by. I approached them, curious myself to learn about these people.

"These elder men were upset with me that I did not address them first when we arrived." Lenai said to me. "I did not show them proper respect." They were Turkana men. Dressed in tattered clothes, they stood with their hands behind their backs. Their language was among the five tribal languages Lenai spoke.

As Lenai got back into their good graces, they repeatedly made the sound *ehi*. It was a crescendo, song-like note that came through with a verbal upswing (eh-EEE). As American English uses the word *yeah*, they used *ehi* to draw the speaker along in conversation. I snickered at the first one, until repetition wore it down to normalcy.

I also noticed that neither man had his two bottom front teeth. Their dentition was poor but this anomaly defied randomness. I inquired directly about this odd pattern.

Lenai paraphrased their response, "All six year old Turkana children have those two teeth pulled. If the child gets lockjaw from a tetanus infection, they can still be fed and therefore survive."

These elderly men were proud of their missing teeth, most notably for advantages gained in the mechanics of spitting. They demonstrated this repeatedly as we chatted on the orange dirt roadside.

The simple fix for our car dragged on. By the time the engine roared back to life, it was five o'clock in the evening. There were only two hours of daylight left. Our tired, scared, and now agitated group had a decision to make. We were two hours short of our destination in Maralal, Samburu district. The path was dirt roads less hospitable by the mile. Should we breakdown again, we could not be sure of our fate.

In light of our travails, the decision to stay was an easy one. The real question was whether to spend the night in Rumuruti, or request the hilltop muzungu to put up a group of unexpected guests. The hotels in Rumuruti were one story shacks used by truckers for sleep and sex before they breached the wilderness of northern Kenya. We could expect accommodations to include noise, insects, filth and a general lack of security. We therefore marched up the muzungu's hill once again.

We came to the gate and got immediate clarification as to the real *risk* behind the fence. Strutting across our eyes with the grace of a prom queen, she wore a coat of light gold with black spots and a thick black line running down from her eye to her chin. She was indisputably a cheetah. The risk warning on the gate now seemed a gross understatement.

John strolled up to the gate. "Don't worry," he said, "Claudia is tame, but she's fickle as a princess."

Knowing the way Murphy's Law permeated the air in Africa, John must have expected us. He showed no surprise at the six foreigners and four Kenyans standing at his doorstep once again. In any case, he was well-prepared to make accommodations.

In a stroke of luck bordering on the miraculous, John and Amanda's business was hosting large groups. They owned a fully functioning campground known as the Bobong Camp-Site. It was even written up in the Lonely Planet guidebook, the bible for travel survival. So, along 120 miles of third world desolation, our car broke down at the foot of a campground written about in the Kenyan guidebook. *Nzuri sana* as they say in Swahili!

John was more than happy to prepare lodges for our stay. The principle structure on the site was a banda, a large cylinder shaped building with a bottom floor and a loft filled with cots and space for our sleeping bags. There were also sinks, cookware, and running water, luxuries akin to fantasy in the African bush.

Standing next to a small circular hut, John continued the tour, "Over here you will find two sit down toilets, it's a glorified outhouse of course, but you won't need to squat. And there you will find two showers. Turn the black handle for hot water."

A chill ran through each of us. Did he say sit down toilets? Hot water? In unison we asked for clarification.

"Yes, we have hot water." He replied. "Make yourselves at home. Let me know if you're in need of anything."

There was no hot water, let alone running water, anywhere on the long journey towards Samburu land. Yet here we were, basking in a magical oasis. Looking around at each of my companions, I saw a sparkle in their eyes, where only the darkest hour can give such a vibrant dawn. It was magnificent. I knew my eyes appeared the same, and I felt it deep in my bones, like I was being watched over from above by a great protector.

We happily distributed the evening's work. The men gathered loose sticks, wood, and boards found around the campsite to build a fire. The ladies cut up tomatoes, onions, potatoes, and carrots. These were wrapped in aluminum foil pouches and buried under the bed of coals burned down from the fire. This food item had many aliases, from Silver Dollars to Hobos. Whatever the name they tasted delicious to our grateful palates.

When night fell in the African bush, it was pitch black across the valley below. But a strange nightlight shone down from the full moon hovering above us. This moon lit up the campsite in a blue haze, casting long shadows across the ground as we sat around the campfire eating, laughing, and generally reveling in the moment. This majestic nighttime atmosphere catapulted to #10 on the LOTIL.

Wei sat next to me and quietly leaned over as she opened her aluminum foil hobo.

"Brian, remember I told you Yin and Yang? You see, here we are. Life have balance."

"It most certainly does, Wei. It most certainly does."

Chinese Condoms and Spring Protection

For the last element of our educational experience in Kenya we were posted at a rural health clinic in Mosoriot, a small town thirty minutes from Eldoret. Our goal was to experience Public Health in rural Africa. Mosoriot was nothing more than a strip of highway 200 meters long with a few small buildings and businesses. It served as a meeting point for thousands of shambas in the Nandi District.

Our group huddled in a small clinic office waiting for Mosoriot's Public Health Officer, a young man named Philip. The lone bookshelf in the office was lined with boxes of condoms. These were handed out for free as part of an agreement between China and Kenya. We were surprised to see such a huge supply still wrapped in cellophane at this rural health clinic.

When Philip arrived, we asked him the story behind these condoms.

"They are Chinese condoms," Philip explained. "They are for the Chinese. I cannot even give them away here. The people say they are too small."

Philip's modesty barely withstood the implications of his statement. We thought it quite amusing. When academicians and politicians argue about giving condoms away in Africa, nobody ever brings up these practical issues of compliance.

Compliance drives another debate in Kenya, and all over Africa. Antiretrovirals, or ARV's, are the drugs that treat HIV infection. They have transformed a universally fatal infection into a chronic disease. They are also the drugs people argue should be given away for free in developing countries.

In Kenya, there is a good infrastructure for distributing ARV's regardless of ability to pay. But if the medicine is not taken continually and consistently, resistant viral strains develop. To prevent resistance, patients are not given ARV's, free or otherwise, unless they show compliance with their drug regimen. As a result, only 10% of known HIV positive patients in Kenya are actually receiving ARV therapy.

Philip didn't talk to us about condoms or ARV's. He served as our field guide to other Public Health efforts taking place in and around Mosoriot. He drove us deep into Nandi District for what he called 'Spring Protection'. There was a natural spring around which they had constructed a flow system, giving rural families access to clean drinking water.

We drove through 20 minutes of rolling farmland, parked the car, and then walked another 15 minutes into a ravine where the spring was located. We came to the bottom of a narrow gulch and found a large concrete structure with two metal pipes extruding from its base. There was water flowing from the pipes, but there was no top to the structure. The stagnant water waiting to flow out was exposed to the surrounding environment.

"You can see the project is not quite finished." Philip said. "We need to cover the reservoir with another concrete slab. We have been waiting on the funding for a year now." He kicked away a dried splattering of bird feces from the concrete base. "And still we wait."

To cover this spring it would cost one U.S. dollar and would take ten minutes to accomplish. This was not about money or resources. It was about organized, thoughtful, political will. None of these does Kenya possess, to the chagrin of heroic laborers like Philip.

There was no one at the well when we arrived, but a trickle of women began appearing. Some had plastic jugs, some carried their children. They came under the auspices of gathering water, but clearly word had spread that muzungus were afoot.

We had fun with these women, blowing up balloons for their children and taking pictures with them. The ones truly seeking water filled their buckets, placed them on their heads and began the slow journey home. For some, this was a mile or more of hilly terrain. Others stayed until we left, sending us off with smiles that expressed gratefulness for breaking the monotony of their day.

On the way back to the clinic, Philip walked us around the main strip of businesses in Mosoriot. The bars, restaurants, and butcheries were nothing more than wooden shacks. There was no electricity, no refrigeration. Raw meat sat in glass boxes to keep them free from flies and filth, which may have worked had the doorframes been closed. Flies swarmed over three day old goat meat, for sale without a discount.

"I have the authority to shut down that butcher," Philip said as we walked back out onto the main highway. "He is in violation of many Public Health codes. But hunger and starvation will take the place of that filthy meat. In Kenya, we must choose our battles wisely."

The Talk

The next week, Philip led us to our final public health endeavor. Accompanied by four Nurse Practitioner students, we walked from the clinic to Mosoriot's all-girls Catholic high school. The grounds of this school consisted of a cattle pasture and six one story elongated buildings. Immediately, we muzungus felt the stares as couplets of girls walked by, whispering to each other before running away, giggling with hands over mouths.

We were there to give a Public Health talk about sexually transmitted diseases, specifically HIV/AIDS. The schoolmaster met us outside and accompanied us into a large schoolroom auditorium. The room was flat and vacuous with a high ceiling and side windows in various states of disrepair.

The students filled row after row of plastic chairs, with more on benches lining the walls. It was quiet as we took our seats in front, facing an audience of at least 200 faces. We had decided on the walk over that I would represent our muzungu faction. I really didn't know what that meant, but my mind was in high gear as the schoolmaster asked this adolescent crowd to give us their undivided attention. Given the topic's sensitive nature, the school officials excused themselves so students could ask questions freely, without fear of rebuke.

My heart pounded as I stared blankly into that sea of white sclera and black skin. I am always nervous before speaking in front of an audience, especially when I haven't prepared. This was certainly going to test my knowledge base about HIV/AIDS. It was one thing to spend an evening reading the chapter on HIV in Harrison's Textbook of Internal Medicine. It was another altogether to teach 200 African teenage girls about it.

The Kenyan nursing students began with the medical side of the talk. They spoke about the virus, how it worked to infect a person, and how it damaged the immune system. One of the students took over the talk and entered a tangent from which he never returned. He spoke in such schooled medical vernacular that I could barely follow it, committing the sacred public speaking foul of not knowing his audience. A glaze came over the eyes of the once excited crowd.

As he gradually lost the audience, my confidence increased. Nervousness even grew into frustration as the student drew up lists of medical complications caused by HIV infection. I caught the eye of another nursing student, who was equally frustrated. She waved her eyes for me to stand up and take over. I nodded and stood up.

A room of eyeballs shot my way, as if a tennis ball had been volleyed towards me. I was violently tossed from my comfort zone, but I was ready to take the responsibility. If Kenya had taught me nothing else, it had taught me to seize the moment. And besides, I had nowhere to take this crowd but up.

Before I spoke, the nursing student who waved me forward stood up as well, saying that it was time to move forward with another portion of the talk. This allowed a graceful exit for the previous speaker.

"I have a question for all of you!" I said. "How do you get the virus called HIV?"

There was quiet. It wasn't clear to the crowd, or to me, if that question was supposed to be answered.

"Let me be more specific," I said, a sense of energy now bubbling up in my own voice. "Can you get HIV from kissing someone?"

I saw heads nod up and down, others nodded back and forth. No one spoke up and I sensed that they might not ever do so in this setting.

"I have an idea," I said. "I want you to take out a pen and paper and write down a question you have about HIV and AIDS. Don't put your name on it; this is totally anonymous."

A few reached for their bags, tearing out paper and pens like I asked. I watched as one small piece of paper crept forward, handed up row by row, until it arrived to me. I unfolded the loose leaf paper.

"Can I get HIV from drinking after someone?" I read aloud. I read it again, and then asked the audience for their thoughts. Still no hands or voices rose up.

I began to fear that my gimmick wasn't catching on. For a split second I remembered back to my eighth grade year when I led my school in the Pledge of Allegiance. I stumbled in the second line before I blanked out completely. There was silence through the microphone. Since then I have occasional moments of performance anxiety that can be quite gripping. Now I was watching an auditorium full of faces teetering on the edge where vibrant expectation slips into disappointment, which is a prelude to total apathy.

"You absolutely cannot get HIV from drinking after someone," I answered. "Sharing a coke with an HIV infected person will not give you the virus."

I scanned across the room as I said this. I could see that I still had their attention. Then another piece of paper was handed to me. Again I unfolded the paper and read aloud.

"Can I get infected by sharing a cigarette?" I asked.

Finally a hand raised by the windows on the far left side! I desperately hoped this was the spark to light the flame. I pointed to her to speak.

"You cannot get HIV by sharing a cigarette or a coke," she said.

"That's right!" I exclaimed. "You've got it!" She could not have imagined my gratefulness for her courage to speak up. "You can only get HIV by blood transfusions or by having sex with another person," I added.

Suddenly, there was a flurry of scribbling in the audience. Papers were passed up faster than I could read them. But I didn't need to read them as hands shot up across the room. Lips and tongues were loosed as these girls began verbally asking their questions. I could see their expectation had in fact turned to full engagement of the topic. Their cultural and personal fears about this strange infection were manifesting in this auditorium.

A girl three rows back stood up to ask her question, "So how can I make sure I never get AIDS?"

What a great question, but how could I summarize that in one sentence? Six hands went up in the audience so I gave her peers the chance to answer. I pointed to the girl furthest back.

"Abstinence," she said.

"Well done," I responded. "Abstinence is the only 100% sure way to protect yourself. Condoms are important if you do have sex, but they're not perfect and they're not always up to you. Abstinence is in your control."

It was a well-timed answer as the schoolmaster re-entered the auditorium. Loosened tongues were bound again. I took my seat and realized how enraptured I had been. My adrenaline was gushing, as if I had been running for a mile.

The schoolmaster, and the students, thanked us for coming. The nursing students set up a table in the front to hand out Aspirin and Tylenol in little brown baggies. Many young girls lined up for these while others filtered outside.

Our muzungu group also went outside and was swarmed by these young girls. They didn't ask us about HIV or anything else we talked about. They wanted pictures with all of us, and they could not stop touching Shira's long, sandy blonde hair. The timid giggles that greeted our arrival were replaced by hugs and waves, the memory of which glares like neon on the background of my Kenya experience.

Israel

Ancient Reunions

After a smooth trip into Tel Aviv on Ethiopian Airlines, I walked through the arrival atrium to catch the southbound train to Beer Sheva. I was delayed a few minutes when, quite suddenly, plain-clothes security materialized out of the busy crowd. From every direction, young men sprinted towards the second floor and out to the parking lot. No doubt they had spotted a suspicious object. Thus I was welcomed back to Israel.

On the LOTIL, train rides are #5. There is much peace in watching the rhythms of land pass across my train window. I was all the more at ease by the Hebrew being spoken around me. My nostalgia was quickly severed by the adjacent Army soldier's M-16 nudging into my left flank. He was a teenager talking on his cell phone, oblivious to my discomfort. I adjusted myself without saying anything, knowing his weapon was still more burdensome to him than to me.

The landscape became more primeval the further south we traveled, entering gradually into the Negev desert. The Old Testament figure, Abraham, roamed this desert and, according to the ancient account in Genesis, established Beer Sheva by making an oath over a well. Today, Israelis come to Beer Sheva for the same reason I did, to work and study at Ben-Gurion University and the ever-expanding Soroka Medical Center. These two institutions employ most of the city in one form or another. In the American sense, Beer Sheva is a college town.

The Paradise Hotel is the nicest and only true hotel in Beer Sheva. Located a mile from Soroka Medical Center and the Medical School for International Health, it was going to be

home for the next two months. Shelley waited for me there as
darkness fell over southern Israel.

I walked through the vacuous and sparsely decorated lobby
straight to the elevators. Children ran everywhere, chased down
by women with short cropped wigs and long dresses. Men in
black hats and long curls of hair running along the sides of their
face were gathered in pockets around the lobby. I caught myself
staring at the festive chaos of this orthodox Jewish wedding,
and even missed a first cycle of elevators because of it. But I
refocused and pushed my way onto the next elevator. Shelley
was waiting. Our two months of separation was about to end.

I knocked on the hotel door and heard the shuffling of feet,
then a door quickly open just inside the room. She was no doubt
in the bathroom taking one last look, an action buried deep in
the genetics of every woman. Every time my family ever took
a road trip home to visit grandparents in Louisiana, my mother
would make us stop two blocks away so she could "put on her
face." I was actually endeared to the practice and thought it was
sweet that Shelley did it now.

When the door opened, there was my beautiful wife. Her
clothes were simple, just jeans and a snug white shirt, but purple
eye shadow colored her upper eyelids and her hair was curled
up where it landed at the shoulders. That was her favorite eye
shadow, and really the only makeup that showed she was wearing
anything at all. Her cheeks held a subtle blush and her lips were
a dulled red. Her hair spoke the most as she only curled it like
that, with a dip at the ends, when she was really trying to look
good. She had been very intentional in preparing for my arrival.

All the makeup and preparation was secondary to the radiance
of her eyes. They were always blue but when her mood was up
they shined. She looked new and fresh to me, the way I saw her
when we first met in college. Back then, if I ran into her on the
LSU campus I would stare at her with investigative eyes. Not
seeking faults, just desiring to know every angle of her face and
neck and shoulders and beyond. I stared at her that way now,

until we embraced. Then it was not a visual remembrance but something in the deeper recesses of my mind. A tactile memory came to life, welling up like dry bones filling with marrow once again. This was the woman I married, but that circumstances had separated for a time.

"I'm so glad you're here." Shelley spoke as we stood there, her head buried in my chest. The curtains were open and Beer Sheva's city lights filtered in, the only lighting in the room.

"This is good, Shelley. I missed you."

"Are you hungry?" she asked, "Do you need anything?"

I just smiled at her, pulling back so I could see her eyes. I was not surprised that so soon after being together she would worry about my needs, and seek to fulfill them.

"I'm okay." I replied.

I kissed her while we stood still close by the door, which had shut on its own. We never turned the lights on that night. Neither did we spend time catching up on everything that had transpired during our separation, or what the next two months in Israel held for us. There was too much to say in that regard, and we would be together from here on out. Nothing would separate us again. It was enough to enjoy that feeling, not looking forward or looking back, to be in the moment, a moment that lasted the entire night.

Clarfield Debate

Truth be told, I have never met a Geriatrician I didn't like. These physicians are uniquely gifted in terms of empathy and interpersonal communication. This was certainly true of the Geriatric Department at Soroka. It was there that I found the most gifted communicator I have ever studied under, a physician named Mark Clarfield.

Dr. Clarfield was short, balding, and entirely unassuming. Canadian by origin, he had eschewed the comforts of Western life to live in Israel. This was to the medical students' benefit, for when he opened his mouth, his self-proclaimed gift-of-gab shone like rays of verbal sunlight.

Our first meeting with Clarfield was ostensibly to introduce the Geriatrics rotation and our curriculum for the coming weeks. But he was far too interesting to get caught up in mundane bureaucracy. He'd rather talk International Health, Cross-Cultural Medicine, or Ethics. This morning we became wrapped in a vigorous discussion about cross-cultural medicine.

"You'll see on this ward," he said, "today even, elderly people with no working knowledge of the local culture or customs, or even of Western culture. These are Jews from Russia, North Africa, Eastern Europe. I make it my business to understand the cultural make-up of these ethnicities."

The state of Israel has a Right of Return policy for any Jew in the world to come live in Israel. The government picks up the tab for all of their social services, including healthcare. This results in many elderly people immigrating to be cared for by the state. They don't speak Hebrew, and they never integrate into the larger society.

From this base, we hotly debated the role of the physician's beliefs in the application of medical care. At one point, Clarfield was cut off by another student. Tension filled the air as we wondered if someone had crossed a forbidden line of disrespect.

"You guys have become so Israeli," he replied, "you don't let anyone finish a sentence."

The tension quickly dissipated, within both Clarfield and the group. Watching him lead this discussion was a work of art.

"Listen," he concluded. "People have beliefs. Our job is not to make them rational. Our job is to work within their beliefs without breaking our own fundamental system."

In one fell swoop, his artful maneuvering of the table debate brought us back into perspective, leaving us a pearl to keep forever.

Yom HaShoa

Our meeting was cut short that morning because of a ceremony at the main University campus. Today was Yom

HaShoa, Holocaust Memorial Day, and there would be musicians and speakers honoring those who perished under Nazi rule so many years ago. I walked over in the late morning to see the event.

I stood on the pedestrian median between the hospital and the University when a loud siren began ringing. It started off in the distance but soon became all-consuming, as though the world was coming to an end. Pedestrians crossing the street came to a stop and stood motionless with their heads bowed. Cars stopped at green lights and driver and passenger all stepped out and did the same.

I looked around me, my curiosity not permitting my eyes to close. I could not find one person moving. Time, as I never imagined it could, stood still, as though the earth stopped rotating or underwent some other cataclysmic pause in the natural order of things. A blanket of stillness permeated all around, pierced by the siren's scream that did not let up. I was actively participating in this memorial service and I am not an Israeli, nor even a Jew. I've never had family who suffered persecution, yet I felt a connection to those around me. A story of suffering that began in the gas chambers of Nazi Germany had reached my heart as well.

When the sirens faded minutes later, heads lifted up and bodies moved, all in complete unison. It was like a movie scene when the director calls for action. I continued on with my day as did everyone else, but with a heaviness of heart that was not present before. I spent the rest of the morning watching holocaust ceremonies at the University. By the time I returned to the hospital that afternoon, the terrible burden of history weighed upon me. I had a hard time focusing. Nevertheless, Dr. Clarfield sent us off to our first Geriatric patient interviews.

I met my patient, Lidia Spiro, at her bedside. Lidia was an 86 year old woman admitted to the ward after breaking her right femur. Such injuries are devastating in the elderly, sometimes even fatal. Lidia was fortunate to be stable and spry despite her injuries.

Perhaps it was my mood after the morning events, or maybe Lidia, like most elderly people, just wanted to tell her story, but we started with the social history instead of the medical one.

"I was a Jew in Poland," she said to me in perfect English, "a city called Grodno. It was the end of 1941. I was 21 years old."

She sat on her hospital bed with her feet on the ground, leaning her hands gently on her four legged walker. Her hands were old bones covered with old skin. Areas of dark pigment spotted the backs of her hands while large veins coursed through like a river. These were deceptive veins, they appeared bulging and full of strength, but sticking a needle in them is like catching a fish with a spear. Any medical student will tell you the trauma caused from fishing around for those veins during blood draws. Thankfully, I was here to interview Lidia, and not to draw her blood.

She said that half the Grodno population was Jewish. It was a centre for Jewish culture. As World War II raged across Europe, Germany took over the Russian controlled portion of Poland, changing her life forever. Jews began dying by the thousands from death squads and pogroms.

"All of the Jews were sent to Ghettos," Lidia said. "Actually, there were two, Ghetto #1 and #2. We were sent to work, some to factories, some to the fields. Now, as time went by we heard news of extermination camps from those who had escaped. We were very scared."

Without another word, Lidia leaned on those old hands of hers and stood up on both feet. She threw the walker out in front of her and started moving away. Was our conversation so quickly over? I didn't ask, instead I got up myself and began walking with her slowly down the breezeway of the geriatric ward. She used the walker adeptly, supporting the hip that surgeons had fixated with screws. I had yet to ask her about that hip, maybe now would be the right time. "How is that…"

"Life was terrible inside the ghetto," she interrupted, though she surely hadn't heard me speak up. "There was no money, no possessions. Everyone was skinny." She stopped her walker as we reached the door leading to the back patio area. She looked at me and held her gaze, wagging her crooked pointer finger gently in the air. "I saw women of great wealth, brought to begging for money on the streets."

I pushed open the door to make way for us outside. The sun was hot but subdued by a haze in the air. We sat on a small wooden bench facing the nursing school.

"There were working ghettos," she continued, adjusting her hospital gown on the short bench. "It was thought that those would last longer." Then she paused. I waited for a moment, but she did not pick up her next sentence even after about ten seconds. I wanted to fill the dead space as my discomfort increased the longer this silence went on, but I fought off this urge. Her eyes were watching something, but I doubted it was the white walls of the nursing school.

Then she turned to me as if no pause had taken place. "I ran away to Bialystok. It was a town very close by with a working ghetto. In Bialystok there was a very strong underground organization. They hid themselves in a nearby forest called Pousha. All runaways tried to get into the forests, as I did." Again her eyes veered away, as though peering into the tree line of her memory.

This time I could not hold my tongue. "What do you mean, 'as you did'? Did you escape into the forest?"

"Actually, I went back and forth from forest to town as a spy. Traps were set by the Germans. They waited and killed many of our people, but the organization was clever, oh they were so clever. We used fake birth certificates of deceased goyim (non-Jews). I used the birth certificate of a Belarusian woman."

"You must have been frightened when a Nazi soldier took your papers."

"Yes, maybe. Frightened is not the right word. Our lives were under such a heavy burden, every moment of every day. Those encounters were..." she paused, "as though the moment of truth had arrived. Whatever happened, the resistance would continue. That gives you great courage."

It actually wasn't hard to imagine Lidia, now with elderly bones and skin, performing such acts of courage. An inner strength poured forth from her eyes and her voice. Even the broken hip succumbed to her will to live and her positive spirit. But she did seem to tire of reliving those moments, and she suddenly turned the question asking around onto me.

"And you, sir, what about you? I live in the past, but you live for today. How did you end up here in Israel? Did you make *Aliyah* (immigrate)?"

"Wait a second, Lidia!" I exclaimed. "What happened in Bialystok? You must tell me! You've brought me this far!"

She shook her head, smiling with a silent chuckle. "You will be a good doctor, and if not, then a journalist. You ask a lot of questions!"

"I've heard that before, Lidia. All my life actually. But especially when people are evading my questions!"

"Yes, of course, I will tell you, but thank God, for my story there isn't much else to say. At war's end, we met the Russians again. I returned to Grodno, but I found nothing was left." She swiped her right arm in front and across her body. "All was destroyed. I had no money of course, but you didn't need a ticket to get anywhere at that time. Everyone was running off to somewhere, so I went to Moscow. There, I began my studies in English and became an English teacher."

Lidia stared at me with a sense of completion in her eyes, looking for satisfaction in mine. She could see my next question brewing. Pleasantly furrowing her brow, she said, "Go ahead. I can see it in your eyes."

She had nailed me spot on. I was a question asker and for somebody like her, I had an endless supply. Each detail in her story only created more questions in my mind. At this point, however, I realized that something very critical was missing in her story.

"Lidia," I began, "you ran off to all these places but you were a young woman."

"Yes. A beautiful young woman!"

"I don't doubt it. But where was your family, your parents, your brothers, your sisters during this whole time."

"For this I can answer you in just one word, Treblinka. All of my family was killed in Treblinka. We were separated when I went to Bialystok. I received news of their capture from friends, and honestly I did not believe it at first. But it was true. They all died there at Treblinka."

Suddenly, I became aware of the sun and the lack of breeze in the air. A drop of perspiration gathered on my forehead, though it wasn't that hot outside, and I deflected my head towards the ground. Lidia, however, showed no discomfort. This was a reality she had lived with for a very long time.

"I came to Israel in December 1991, after my husband died." She said. "I realized I felt no sense of ownership over my place, the land I was in. So I came to Israel." She looked at me carefully, as though this was the only point that mattered. "This is the only home for the Jew."

Leaning back, she inhaled deeply and smiled, "All these questions of yours, don't you want to know about my hip?"

I laughed and replied, "Yes, of course, Lidia. Now, how about that hip of yours?"

Hummus Lawn and the Box-Break-Down Guy

I left the Geriatric Ward at 4:30 PM that afternoon. I had spent about an hour and a half with Lidia, and she stayed on my mind as I left the floor. Outside, the biblical hot winds known as hamsin had arrived in full and were kicking up dust. The hazy atmosphere had thickened since the early afternoon when Lidia and I sat outside. Now the air was tinged yellow and coated with sand. I could stare straight at the sun, which looked like the optic disc of a human retina, a fluorescent glowing ball in a beige sky.

To get home from the Geriatric Department, I crossed the center of the hospital grounds. It was an open lawn the size and shape of a football field. Concrete paths crisscrossed the green and were traversed by patients, doctors, nurses, janitors, and food carts. Sprawled out in clusters around the lawn were the Arab Bedouins. They poured in from the greater reaches of the Negev desert to either deliver babies or treat their children.

Bedouin men lay outstretched on the lawn, crossing their legs scissor-like below them while twirling prayer beads in habitual rhythm. They were as comfortable on the ground as my grandfather in his Lazy-Boy. Women sat with their children in their own circles around tubs of hummus, stacks of pita bread, and plastic bags full of juice, soda, and chocolate wafers. Eating hummus is a communal activity, like drinking mate in Argentina. I never walked by without having the urge to introduce myself and take a swipe of hummus with them.

I passed by an elderly Bedouin couple, the woman walking three feet behind her husband. The man was a caricature from a Near East Anthropology textbook. He wore the common white head scarf bound by six black strands. A brown leather belt held tight his long white gown, and a leather extension ascended over his chest. A traditional knife flashed as he swung his arms in gait, tucked in a decorative sheath under his belt. He finished off the outfit with a navy blue suit jacket.

They barely acknowledged each other, or me, as I sped past. As I rounded the Café Aroma and the outdoor elevators of the Internal Medicine building, I saw a familiar face. It was a face known at Soroka since my first days of medical school, almost five years ago. I didn't know his name, but in my mind I referred to him as the Box-break-down guy.

A pot-bellied thirty-something hospital employee with a dark black scraggly beard, he'd been collecting cardboard boxes, breaking them down into flat pieces, and discarding them in that same dumpster for years. The temporal distance I had experienced from Israel was dismantled like one of those boxes. This man's continued presence at this station of life made it clear that I'd hardly left at all. While life may have seemed long, indeed it was not.

I thought back to Joe in New York City. The static life of the Box-break-down guy was like Joe's C-Span marathons every night in that small hostel basement. These patterns developed over time, an offspring of life circumstances and the repetitive nature of the rising and setting of the sun every day. Change was possible but not without a purposeful and committed act of individual will.

I held a deep seated fear that my life would become stuck like theirs in a revolving door of bland repetition. That I will wake up everyday and experience the same four walls in some office, the same tastes, smells, sights, and sounds day in and day out until my best years are spent. My mind is in constant rebellion against such inertia, refusing to let my life take that shape, or to continue in it. That drive led me to a medical school in the Middle East, and to a curriculum that would send me farther still. I would never live my life, for richer or poorer, for better or worse, like Joe or the Box-break-down guy.

The Superhero Whistler

The Memory Clinic is located at Soroka's psychiatric hospital facility. A morning visit was a requirement of our geriatrics rotation. Like most psychiatric hospitals, it is located at the edge of town, far away from the central medical center. Our group congregated early in the morning with the day's attending physician. He informed us with a straight face that all our scheduled patients had forgotten their appointments. Maybe he could still bring one in, but it would take a few hours.

My morning suddenly open, I sat at the open-air café where the psychiatric patients pass their days. For people-watching, nothing compares to the grounds of a Psychiatric hospital. It falls at #9 on the LOTIL.

Patients constantly walk around as a result of akathisia, an unfortunate side effect of antipsychotic medications that leaves them with an irresistible urge to move. I watched one man walk straight ahead, never veering from the path made by his eyes that stared rigidly at the ground. When he came to a person or other barrier in his path, he changed direction and continued walking, completely straight.

"Isaac! Isaac!" Another patient called out to him. Isaac stopped in his tracks and, without altering his heavy gaze, mumbled, "What? What?"

The other man yelled out inquiries regarding Isaac's identity as the Jewish Messiah. Isaac stood frozen in place. Only when the taunts ended did Isaac un-stick himself. He continued his walking, in a perfectly straight line.

The café was a barrage of unpredictable speech and action. I was soon joined at my table by a short, heavy-set woman dressed in all black. She wore dark sunglasses even in the shade. She did not introduce herself, or even ask if she could sit down.

"Everyone is jealous of me," she began. "They are jealous because I am so beautiful. My eyes are so beautiful in the sun, they sparkle. I have to wear sunglasses because everyone is jealous of how beautiful my eyes are."

My participation in this conversation was clearly optional from this woman's perspective. She continued, "But now everyone is even jealous of my sunglasses. You see how beautiful my sunglasses are."

I nodded kindly. I tried not to over-affirm their beauty, lest I become one of the jealous ones.

Leaning over the table, she said, "A religious woman put her hands on my belly and told me that God has put six children in my womb." She counted off 1 through 6, each time patting herself on her belly.

"I am frustrated," she continued. "I have been carrying them around for so long!" The corners of her mouth began to quiver and tears fell below her sunglasses.

"It has been years now!" she exclaimed. I thought she was imploring me to do something. But it was not from me she was seeking help.

"When is God going to take these children out?" she pleaded.

I gripped my lips together tightly and looked at her with sympathy. I was at a loss on how to comfort this 'gravid' woman. As I moved my head in sympathetic nods, my attention was drawn away by a patient I recognized from my third year psychiatric rotation. I excused myself from the lamenting woman in her 124th week of gestation, giving chase to this unforgettable character, a schizophrenic named Fabio.

Fabio was a permanent resident of the psychiatric ward, this being his fifteenth year. He was a schizophrenic for whom modern drugs had failed miserably. While his prognosis was poor, he had little displeasure with the grandeur of his life, most notably expressed by the décor of his bedroom.

Plastered over every space of wall was a combination of sex, piety, and poetic expression. Magazine cut-outs of hard core pornography filled up most of his de-facto wallpaper. Women did unspeakable acts to men, and vice-versa. Fabio claimed these depictions expressed God's beauty and power.

Checkered throughout the graphic sexual images were more magazine cut-outs, these depicting pious religious leaders. The pope was a favored icon, as well as Orthodox Jewish rabbis. Whatever space was not occupied by the aforementioned was filled with torn out notebook pages of Fabio's personal poetry and drawings. The handwriting was childlike and the drawings like kid art. The entire spectacle was a disturbing contrast of both repulsion and fascination.

Today, Fabio wore a white naval officer's cap. His shirt was a military green button down. It was un-tucked and had a button missing at the bottom. It would fly open with the wind, exposing the grey hair on his belly. A light green beret was tucked under a military shoulder bar. His beard was shaggy and dark grey. He was a cross between Fidel Castro and Saddam Hussein, the way he appeared when dragged out of that spider hole by the U.S. military.

"Fabio! Fabio!" I called after him. He turned around and waited for me to catch up.

He recalled me only faintly, which in any case was irrelevant. As with the pregnant woman, my role in the conversation was to stand there.

Fabio whispered to me, motioning his finger over his mouth to let me know it was not safe to speak too loudly, "Listen, friend, there are conspiracies around here. You must not speak this to anyone else. They try their manipulations on me, everyone does. But I am the King. You know this of course. I am the King over all the leaders in the world."

He raised his hand chest high, pointing his palm outward towards me. He counted on his fingers, "George Bush, Bill Clinton, Ariel Sharon. I know them all. They are all in the palm of my hand."

With head lowered and eyebrows raised, he stared up at me like my fourth grade teacher driving a point home.

"You understand?" he continued. "The people here, they know and they try to manipulate me."

I nodded my head and morbidly enjoyed Fabio's wild version of reality. He took me by the shoulder and we sat on a bench near the inpatient psychiatric ward where he lived. I asked him what significance the Green Beret held. He threw his hands and head back and then came in close to me, again putting his hand on my shoulder.

"I am the head of a secret intelligence agency." He said, swiveling his head around scanning for eavesdroppers.

"It is a group more clandestine than the Mossad," he said. Then he sat back, swiveling his head again, satisfied I had received this confidential information.

The Mossad is Israel's notorious equivalent to the U.S. Central Intelligence Agency. This group tracked down the famous Nazi war criminal Adolf Eichmann and carried out the assassination of those responsible for the massacre at the 1972 Olympic Games in Munich.

Then I remembered something interesting about Fabio's version of reality.

"Fabio, can you still communicate with the birds?" I asked.

Proudly, Fabio broke into a loud and fluctuant whistle. His cheeks sucked in and out with concentration and fervor.

As he performed on his own grandiose stage, a classmate passed by waving for me to return to the Memory Clinic. A patient had apparently remembered their appointment.

I turned back to Fabio, who was moving his arms wildly with the song.

"I have to go now, Fabio. I'm so glad I got to talk to you!" I said.

Fabio paid no attention and followed me as I walked away, yelling, "You see the power I have. The birds, I communicate with them. You have seen!"

He stopped in his tracks and continued ranting, "I am both Superman and Spiderman in one human being. I am amazing, you see!"

He spread his legs and did toe-touch stretches, proof he was limber enough for any Superhero task.

Yerushalayim

Three weekends into our stay Shelley and I found pressing reasons to visit the heartbeat of Israeli society, the holy city of Jerusalem. Shelley had been contracted to write a status report on the negotiations between the Israelis and Palestinians regarding the Gaza disengagement. She was scheduled to meet with the head of the Palestinian Authority's Negotiation Support Unit, Mein Erekat.

Erekat's office was in Ramallah, the de facto Palestinian Capital in the West Bank very near to Jerusalem. Nizar greatly assisted the logistics of our trip by offering a stay in his family's home in Al-Ram, a nearby town. He wanted to fulfill his promise in Kenya that I see Palestinian life in the West Bank, a place that'd be difficult, if not dangerous, to venture into alone.

That Friday morning the open air Egged Bus Station in Beer Sheva was filled to the brim with young soldiers heading home for the weekend from their southern military stations. Egged is Israel's national bus line and the only public transport to Jerusalem. Kiosks lined the loading area selling raw nuts, shwarma, falafel, chicken schnitzel, and pizza. I bought my favorite travel snacks: cashews, chocolate cake-in-a-bag, and vanilla flavored milk.

We rode through the northern Negev desert parallel with the train tracks I came in on. When those tracks pushed west, we coursed northeast where arid desert gave way to steep hills with pine and olive trees sprouting from rock-scattered soil. The final approach to Jerusalem made me dizzy with the great rise and fall of the roadway. It was clear why the Bible always speaks of 'going up' to Jerusalem.

Our destination was the downtown Jerusalem bus station, a mega-station with security comparable to a small airport. After descending the bus, we walked through an archway metal detector before being scanned by a security guard wielding a paddle shaped detector.

"Do you have a weapon?" He asked in Hebrew. This is a standard question and, given the heavily armed population, it is justified. I then placed my bag on a conveyor belt, where X-ray images scanned the contents of my personal effects. Passing successfully, we were set free to enjoy the sights and sounds of Jerusalem.

Shelley and I found a city bus headed toward Zion Square. There were no security checks on these buses. Heading down

Jaffa Street, the main drag towards Jerusalem's Old City, I stared intently at each group of boarding passengers.

Jewish boys with fringe tassels hanging down from under their shirts stood next to their tall, strong jawed fathers who wore dark beards and fur caps. The other passengers were secular Israelis, students, soldiers, or tourists. As I profiled each one, I remembered the psychological vigilance that defines life in Jerusalem. Police and soldiers were visible at every bus stop, but they brought me little comfort. However low the risks of terrorists bombing my bus, it was a very real threat. Nothing could assuage that fear.

For those who know Jerusalem history, riding down Jaffa Street is like passing through a memorial ground. We passed Mahane Yehuda Market to the right, a labyrinthine fruit and vegetable market that has seen many Palestinian suicide bombers enter its stalls, and many dead and dismembered carried away as a result. Further down we crossed the intersection of Jaffa and King George Street, cornered by the Sbarro pizza restaurant. Terrorists made this pizza joint a memorial for 15 civilians on August 9, 2001. Almost half the victims were children.

Then we came to Zion Square. This epicenter of West Jerusalem tourist shops is the preferred site for Palestinian suicide bombers. In December 2001, two suicide bombers detonated themselves in the middle of the Square. Chaos ensued. Ambulances descended on the area. Then a parked car burst into shards and flames. Deaths were in the double digits and close to 200 were injured. At this stop we disembarked.

Tmol Shilshom

Unless you are told about it, you'll never find Tmol Shilshom café. It is veiled by a façade of Jerusalem Stone walls and small shops selling handmade pottery and calligraphy. As was our habit, Shelley and I took lunch and a rest at this enchanted café.

We shimmied our way through the creaky front door and scanned for a seat. We found a small table in the back of the café with two wood chairs. Hidden nails poked my back if I reclined too far, but the smooth maroon suede backing compensated for having to sit erect.

The window to our backs peered out onto Zion Square. Otherwise, we were surrounded by books. Every crevice that allowed for nails and wood, and even niches cut out of the wall, were lined with shelves holding Hebrew, English, German, and Russian titles. Some were old and used, while others were still wrapped in cellophane.

We ordered some coffee and lunch and started reading. I had a book with me, *A Prayer for Owen Meany* by John Irving, but I ended up pulling three other books off the shelf.

"Oh, brother," Shelley said as my stack grew higher, "that's starting to look like your bedside table." My curiosity far exceeds the speed at which I read and so I haven't finished a book from start to finish in years. My bedroom is always littered with half-read paperbacks, which to this day I have every intention of reading.

After our food came, Shelley looked up at me and I was very surprised to see a hint of red at her bottom eyelid with a small welling of tears. Shelley despises making public scenes or exposing her emotions in front of strangers. I put my fork down. She had my undivided attention before she even said a word.

"Promise me you'll never leave again."

"What do you mean?"

"I haven't said anything about it," she said, wiping the first escaping tear from her cheek. "I've just been happy to be with you again."

"Shelley, did I do something wrong?"

"I know this didn't come across through email or the letters I sent you, but I was really miserable in Boston."

"What do you mean, miserable? What happened?"

"It was lonely." She leaned forward wanting to emphasize her point without raising her voice or letting the tears pour out.

"I got sick and tired of coming home to nothing. I felt like a single girl, worse than a single girl, what was mine I didn't even have."

"I'm sorry, I didn't realize. I mean, I know it was hard on you. But you know I couldn't help it. Kenya was part of my curriculum."

"And Montana?"

"Oh. Goodness, this is not about the last two months, this is about the last year."

"Of course it is. How much have we been together this last year?"

I didn't address this question because the answer wasn't a pretty one. I just looked down at the open book on the small circular table in front of me. I felt as low as I could be. I had not sensed the space created between us from our time apart, but clearly it was there.

"I didn't have much say in all this." I said. "Montana, yes, that was on me. But this fourth year was why I came to med school here. How could I not take advantage of it?"

"Was it worth it? Was it worth us being separated?"

My lips felt like they'd been smacked and were now useless, without any power to respond. I looked around the café, but I could see no sanctuary for me. I was in a hole I could not climb out. "How can I answer that question, Shelley?"

"It's not hard. Was your experience in, wherever, Montana, Kenya, New York even, was it worth having your wife feel like she didn't have a husband?"

"I didn't realize I was trading one for the other." A defensive posture crept into my voice. I knew that would not take us down the road to healing. "I would never want you to feel abandoned. But you know I don't see life that way."

"I know how you see life. I know you grew up saying goodbye all the time. But you know that I didn't. Besides, remember that I was the one at home while you were out traveling the world."

"Just so you know, this part of my fourth year, the part I get to share with you, has been what I longed for since my first night in the youth hostel in New York. I always prefer being with you than being without you. You know this."

"I know you do, and now I need you to be with me, and promise me that you won't leave me again. Ever. I don't want to feel single. I want to feel married."

"We're back together, Shelley," I said, taking her hand from across the table. I rubbed my finger over her wedding ring, a subtle line of seven small diamonds. "I don't know what's in store for us, but I can promise you a three year respite in residency. I won't be going anywhere about 80 hours of every week."

"Good. You deserve it." She broke a slight smile. I was never so grateful for her good disposition, or that she understood me enough to forgive me. This fourth year journey was my own doing, if only for choosing the MSIH program and for taking advantage of every opportunity to travel and be in strange and uncomfortable environments. I had given little consideration to the potential costs involved, like trading exotic strangers for my wife. I may not have viewed it as such, but I certainly understood Shelley's perspective in this regard.

The waiter came to bus our plates from lunch. Dressed like a kibutznik in a maroon shirt with a cut out collar, he stood by our table placing plates into a dirty dish bin, all the while eavesdropping on the table next to us. A young woman speaking in a thick Israeli accent was raising her voice, "...for a naïve vision of peace they are giving up hard land..." Our waiter began shaking his head before turning back towards our table.

"Some people do not understand the path to peace," he said under his breath. He began wiping down our table with a white towel. His interruption redirected our thoughts.

"So, what brings you to this lovely country of ours?" he asked, looking at me. I told him that I studied medicine in Beer Sheva.

"Beer Sheva? We should give that place back to the Arabs!" he exclaimed. "Do you think I mind giving up Beer Sheva for peace? I will give up the Golan too, for peace with Syria." His voice attracted the attention of the café manager, who approached our table as well.

"It will be easier to give up the Golan than it was to give up the Sinai," the manager said. His head was shaved and he wore a dark five o'clock shadow on his face. "I was one years old when we gave up the Sinai; that's where my parents lived. The Sinai was protection for Israel. And we gave it up. The Golan is not Israel. Everyone knows that. If (Syrian President) Assad wants peace with Israel, the people will believe him. And they will give up the Golan, you will see. It is a matter of time only."

Our table of a kibutznik waiter, a pacifist café manager, and two American Christian gentiles hotly debated Lebanon and the promised Syrian exit, the Iraq war and the motives behind it, and about the Palestinians and a true peace. Our small talk, like everything else in Jerusalem, was heavier than lead. It created a physical tension in the air, as if the walls of the Old City were really magnets, pulling on everything within and around us, even on the words from our lips.

Nizar, the Wall, and the ZAKA cleanup

By sunset we were rested from our stop at Tmol Shilshom and had finished browsing the shops of Zion Square. It was time to meet up with Nizar. Dusk quickly faded to darkness as our cab arrived at the Beit Chanina checkpoint. A long line of red taillights preceded the white lights emanating from the concrete border crossing. We got out and approached on foot.

We passed through a seven foot high metal turnstile, the only barrier to our direct entrance into Palestinian territory. Nizar was waiting for us in his car. We drove only a few minutes to his house, a beautiful multi-story building made of Jerusalem stone. Between Nizar's home and downtown Ramallah was Kalandia checkpoint station, another entrenchment of the Israeli military a few miles deeper into Palestinian territory. While only a ten minute drive, crossing that checkpoint could take hours on a bad day.

We left very early the next morning. Yellow and orange taxis lined the roadsides for a half mile leading to the Kalandia gate. We parked the car and footed across the checkpoint. Walking across the checkpoint towards Ramallah, no one checked our identification.

On the other side, I stopped to look around. I wanted to absorb the feeling and the sight of Palestine. There was busyness in the air. People walked everywhere while cars, mostly taxis, crept along, scavenging for passengers.

To my immediate left was a large concrete tower. Encircling the mushrooming top of the tower was a narrow window eight inches thick and as impenetrable to bullets as it was to vision. Flowering out of the window band was a large and ominous machine gun. It reminded me of the twigs hanging out of Maria's ears in my New York apartment and was connected to an equally dark world inside. The machine gun cast its shadow on all who traversed the checkpoint.

The concrete tower initiated an equally portentous structure. Emanating from the side opposite the checkpoint was a concrete wall. It stood at least twenty feet high. Slab after slab of concrete stood erect, like soldiers in formation, for as far as the eye could see. In Israel, it is known as the Security Fence, purposed to keep suicide bombers out of Israeli territory. For Palestinians, it is simply the Wall, one more reminder of the suffocating presence of a powerful enemy.

There was nothing aesthetic about its form. The only décor was black spray-painted graffiti, mostly in Arabic and illegible to my eye. I did see one line in English. In large capital letters near the base of the wall was written, *Fuck all Jews*.

Following Nizar's lead, we climbed into a taxi and started for Mr. Erekat's office. The first area we passed was Kalandia

Refugee Camp. A U.N. camp established in 1949, it is now a full fledged city, with apartment complexes, homes and shops. Were it not for the name, and for the worn down U.N. Headquarters at the entrance to the area, I would not have known it was filled with a displaced people.

The Palestinian Authority's Negotiation Support Unit is located in Al-Bireh, a sister municipality to Ramallah. Nizar and I dropped Shelley off at the office, and then doubled back to Ramallah. We got out at Ramallah Friends School, a Quaker institution where Nizar attended high school.

"See that building over there," he began, "do you remember the Israeli soldiers that got lynched? That's the building, right next to my high school."

That lynching was an early event in the intifada which began a few months after I arrived in Israel in the fall of 2000. Two IDF soldiers were caught in Ramallah and arrested by Palestinian Police. They were taken to the Police Station where a mob attacked and killed the two soldiers, mutilating the bodies and dragging at least one through the Ramallah streets. One of the attackers leaned out of the second floor window displaying his blood stained palms to the frenzied crowd below. That picture ran on front pages across the globe. The look of jubilee on his face I never forgot.

"The Israeli army destroyed it." Nizar continued. "They fired a missile that missed the building and hit my mom's classroom."

Nizar's mode of speech was matter of fact, and just a shade above monotone. Even when telling something so personally offensive as his mother's classroom taking a direct missile hit, he remained calm and consistent.

Continuing towards the downtown hub, tall buildings gave the city a metropolitan feel. There were signs everywhere for shops and businesses, and advertisements for all kinds of products. Men dressed like Turks in red fez hats sold tea from silver urns strapped to their backs. Street life was vibrant with the hustle and bustle of commerce.

Nizar stopped at a street vendor and bought us a three shekel kebab (US$0.70) shoved into pita bread.

"I got an email yesterday from that Kenyan girl I dated." He said. "She said she converted to Christianity, she was feeling so guilty about being with me."

"Nizar, you're like a missionary!" I replied. "Who knew that sleeping with you could be a spiritual experience?"

"Maybe your church could send me out to spread the message," he said. A deviant smile on his face was as vibrant an expression his muscles would allow.

Approaching the epicenter of Ramallah, we passed under an archway that served as a large billboard for advertisements. The current advertisement was for no commercial product. On pitch black background, gold letters read, *Save Jerusalem Against the Israeli Wall and Settlements.* It was a simple political propaganda to rouse support and action from the populace.

This was only a harbinger of the rhetoric I was about to see. Through the archway we opened into the frantically busy downtown center, the convergence point for the city's main streets. There was a monument in the middle which cars and pedestrians circled around. The sides of entire buildings were covered with huge signs perpetuating various political angles. It was Times Square with Arabic script and a tumultuous political obsession.

There were multiple large scale displays of Marwan Barghouti, a hero to Palestinians for his violent efforts against Israel. He is currently bouncing around Israeli prisons for those acts. One of the pictures showed him giving a speech before a microphone, while another showed him with his handcuffed hands raised victoriously above his head. They were huge pictures and emotionally gripping.

The largest image was a young Palestinian man dressed in green military clothing. He wore a black bandana and held a machine gun in each arm. The butt of the guns rested on his hips and pointed out. On the side of the display there was a filmstrip with six small inset pictures. I couldn't make them out until I saw smaller scale flyer versions plastered everywhere around town.

Each small picture was taken from various aspects of a suicide bombing either directed or carried out by the gun-toting martyr in the main image. The first scene was after the bombing, a twisted scrap of metal visible in the background. It was the bus that minutes before was carrying Israeli mothers, children and otherwise innocent civilians.

The focus of the picture was Israel's special clean up unit, ZAKA. This volunteer squad of Orthodox Jews is the one seen on CNN walking around every terrorist crime scene. They gather up pieces of flesh and body parts, even spilt blood, for proper Jewish burial.

The next picture was a body bathed in blood lying on a gurney pushed by Israeli medics towards an ambulance. The man pushing the gurney held an I.V. bag while screaming at someone in the distance. The final picture was an Israeli man in the same street scene, his white shirt soaked with blood, his face torqued with pain. His lips were drawn back, mouth open with his eyebrows raised, and the lines on his face were thick from tense, emotional pain. He looked distraught and desperate.

More than any other, this picture disturbed me. I was sure he lost someone he loved. Perhaps he had put his daughter onto that bus and was watching it pull away when his world exploded. She was obliterated. His soul was destroyed. This was terrorism and it was glorified in the Ramallah city square.

Palestinians seem trapped under delusions of victory through a form of violence difficult to rationalize. And yet even my own impressions of Palestine were dominated by the Israeli presence: the checkpoints, the glaring machine gun, the Wall that suffocates the people on this side of it. I empathized with Nizar, moderate enough to study medicine in Israel, even while his family suffered missile strikes and the lack of national identity known to all levels of Palestinian society. But, the situation doesn't exist in a vacuum, with one side purely oppressing another. Palestine needs a Gandhi, or a Martin Luther King, Jr., someone to resist in a way that would melt hearts and minds, instead of blowing them up.

Nizar and I ate lunch and then met up with Shelley, who had since been taken by Erekat's driver to the Palestinian Authority's main compound in Ramallah, known as the Mukata'a. We spent a few minutes at Yasser Arafat's tomb, which was next to the parking lot of this compound, and then made our way back to Jerusalem.

Sagiv the Settler

The sun was just waking up in Beer Sheva on the first morning of my next rotation, Anesthesiology. Walking past the strip mall between the Paradise Hotel and the main road to Soroka, I was surprised to be confronted by the vibrant blue eyes of the sui generis Family Physician, Dr. Sagiv.

Many doctors, usually of surgical persuasions like Dr. Upchurch in Montana, have a nervous energy about them. Their eyes are intense, their limbs in constant motion. Sagiv's energy, while overwhelming, befit a Family Physician who wore a stethoscope around his neck and a handgun on his hip. He was a settler in Gaza.

Settlements are areas of Jewish habitation within otherwise Palestinian controlled territory. These are typically small, fully functioning townships that are fortified and guarded heavily by the Israeli military. Their presence reflects the Zionist spirit envisioning Israeli sovereignty over all the land in Gaza and the West Bank. It is a constant source of tension between Israel and the Palestinians.

Sagiv drove in from Gaza, 30 minutes from Beer Sheva, to moonlight a few shifts every month in the Soroka Emergency

Room. I met him while rotating through as a third year medical student. He was Canadian by origin and loved to teach, making him easy to befriend.

After I dropped hints of my interest, Sagiv invited me to visit the settlement where he'd been living for the last 20 years. Neve Dekalim was part of Gush Katif, the largest settlement block in all of Gaza. His family had been there for two generations.

I shadowed him in his clinic, and as he performed a Brit Milah circumcision ceremony in the community. My jaw hit the floor when, after cutting the infant's foreskin, he placed his mouth over the penis and sucked off the blood. Nobody else grimaced, so I took it as a historic, if not odd, religious practice. I would have appreciated forewarning for such a practice, and I let Sagiv know as much.

Later during my visit, we took lunch at his home and were interrupted by machine gun fire. Sagiv put his fork down and placed his walkie-talkie onto the open table. It beeped and he took a report from the field, which was the settlement's perimeter fence a few hundred yards away. Military sirens zoomed past the house.

Some Arabs were caught infiltrating the fence, but there were no injuries. He put the walkie-talkie down, picked up his spoon, and continued eating as if nothing had happened.

I saw Sagiv once on television while I was home in the U.S. There was another infiltration of the fence, this time successful. A number of settlers were dead. Sagiv was on CNN rushing a gurney to a waiting ambulance.

At the present moment, Israel's Prime Minister, Ariel Sharon, had ordered the dismantling and evacuation of all Gaza settlements. The reaction among the general Israeli populace was fierce, both for and against the withdrawal. The opposition visually unified their struggle using the color orange, a tactic borrowed from the successful Orange Revolution in the Ukraine protesting their fraudulent 2004 presidential election. Orange flags, ribbons, and stickers were seen all over Israel. Sharon's proposal threatened to displace Sagiv and his family.

"Sagiv, how is everything?" I asked. "Are ya'll worried about evacuating Gaza?"

"It's not gonna work, *Baruch HaShem*," he replied, invoking a call to God himself in the matter. "The government has threatened before and they never follow through." He swayed back and forth as he spoke, constantly shifting his body weight. I noticed an orange Lance Armstrong Live Strong bracelet on his left wrist.

"If they do," he continued, "they'll probably put us in a refugee camp somewhere."

How would he rebuild his life should he be expulsed from his home and practice? Would he relocate to a West Bank settlement? I had so many questions, but Sagiv was in a hurry this morning to meet a visiting colleague at the hotel.

"Shabbat Shalom (Peaceful Sabbath)," he bid me as he went on his way.

Darin the Thai Laborer

An important aspect of Anesthesiology is the critical care patient. Therefore, we spent a number of days in Soroka's Medical Intensive Care Unit, or MICU. Dr. Jacoby was the MICU attending during our rotation through this unit. A tall Israeli man, he was easily distinguished by his plump cheeks. They looked like a chipmunk storing acorns. We accompanied him each day on morning rounds.

Bed after bed was a similar scene. The patients lay flat on their back, tubes emanating from every orifice; the mouth, the nose, and the catheter that snaked out by the legs. If their eyes were open, they stared off into space. Breathing was disturbingly rhythmic as their lungs were inflated like balloons by the ventilator machine next to the bed. This accordion in a glass tube squeezes and then relaxes in relation to the rise and fall of the patient's chest. These patients were in a holding cell, inexpressive and immobile, waiting for anything to either spark them back to life or defeat the machines and find permanent rest and peace.

Bed number seven held a small framed man wearing only a neck-brace. He was not breathing through a machine, though he did wear an Oxygen mask. His eyes were active.

"This is Darin," a resident said in Hebrew, presenting the patient to Dr. Jacoby. "A 41 year old male, migrant worker from Thailand, generally in good health, he fell from a height three days ago, receiving a bilateral facet dislocation at C6 through C7. Screws were placed to stabilize the fracture. He is now a paraplegic, and also has difficulty moving his right arm."

I leaned over to a nurse and inquired whether or not this Thai patient spoke Hebrew or English. She told me he spoke English.

Dr. Jacoby interjected the resident's presentation with questions about the patient's breathing and other parameters of his organs and blood. Once reassured the patient was stable, the group moved to the next bed. Darin was expressionless throughout the team's discussion of his grave prognosis.

My mind did not let go of this paralyzed man. His neck was broken, his legs nothing but dead weight. His arms would never be normal strength. I stayed behind to speak with him for a moment.

"Hi, Darin," I said. "My name is Brian Neese. I'm a medical student here. How are you?"

He shook his head, clearly not understanding what I had said. I leaned over and repeated myself. Again he shook his head.

"Darin, do you speak English?" I received another blank look.

Darin clearly did not speak English. I repeated myself in Hebrew and he didn't understand that either. If he didn't understand either of those languages, how did the nurse tell him that he was never going to walk again? How did she ask him where his family was, or how to contact them? How did she answer any questions he might have about spending the rest of his life in a wheelchair? I approached the nurse, but she maintained that he did speak English. She continued prepping the I.V. medications in front of her, signaling she was too busy to have this conversation.

A classmate on rounds told me of a Thai speaker in our program, Miriam Rahav. I was not altogether surprised by this fact as my class of thirty students covered seventeen languages with fluency. With Miriam's help, we took matters into our own hands.

The next morning, she came with me to Darin's bed in the far corner of the Unit. Miriam spoke to Darin with a soft voice in his native tongue. I waited for his eyes to light up and start shouting with joy that someone was finally communicating with him. He did neither of these. He responded to Miriam's questions calmly, without a change in facial expression.

They went back and forth in Thai, but Darin's voice was muffled by his Oxygen mask. To hear him better, she took the mask in her hands and pulled it towards the top of his head. Abruptly, she caught herself midway and paused. She remembered it was disrespectful to touch a Thai person's head. The head was considered the physical and spiritual apex of the person. Darin then gave permission to place the mask on his forehead, since there was nothing else to do.

I was filled with pride at that moment, knowing our program trained physicians like Miriam. She understood the complexity of cross-cultural medicine, and the importance of addressing Darin's needs based on his culture and belief systems. That is the mission of my medical school, and I was watching its fulfillment before my very eyes.

"Does he remember what happened to him?" I asked. "Is he aware what is happening now?"

Darin remembered falling off a ladder at his worksite. He didn't remember much after that, just waking up in the hospital. He assumed he'd feel better in a few days and go back to work.

My worst fear was true. Darin didn't know he was paraplegic. In a country whose language he did not speak, and a culture he barely understood, he had no one to advocate for, or emotionally support him. We decided to bring Dr. Jacoby over. He should deliver the news to Darin, and explain to him the extent of his injury.

Dr. Jacoby was listening to residents present their patients on morning rounds. I interrupted him as they transitioned from one comatose patient to the next. Dr. Jacoby listened intently while I explained the extraordinary circumstances of our Thai patient. He agreed with my request, and moved on to the next patient.

I should not have expected him to drop everything and run to Darin's bedside, but our translator was skipping out on her own responsibilities to be there. Not to speak of the flagrant human rights violation the last three days had been for Darin, having no information regarding his condition. Rounds continued.

Two mechanical lungs later, I stopped Dr. Jacoby again, this time my voice quivering as I urged him to see the patient in bed number seven. Dr. Jacoby once again agreed. When the group left the bedside, I stepped in front of Dr. Jacoby, physically reminding him of his promise.

After reviewing the case briefly, Dr. Jacoby spoke to Miriam for her to translate. "We expect improvement," he said, "but he'll have difficulty getting the strength back in his legs." He did not speak directly to Darin, neither in verb tense or eye contact.

With that, Dr. Jacoby and his group of residents and nurses moved on. He didn't wait for Darin to internalize the information, to ask questions about his condition, or if he wanted help contacting his family. There was also no explanation that when he became stable enough, the State of Israel would send him back to Thailand.

Miriam and I talked with Darin some more, but since we couldn't expound on his medical status, we let his false hopes for a full recovery linger. We did ask about his family in Thailand and learned that he had a wife and two small children. He didn't want them to know about his condition because they'd be devastated.

"If he goes back to Thailand he will not survive," Miriam told me quietly. "There's no social services, no safety net for him there. If he's wheelchair bound, there'll be no wheelchair and no one to push him around. His family could help, but in poverty someone has to do something for food. It will be a desperate situation."

So that was Darin's future. Miriam promised to come back and visit him, and he could call on her to come by anytime, day or night. We left the MICU laden with the heavy yoke of things we could not change.

Ze'ev Shabbat

Every stop in my Fourth Year journey crossed paths with characters so unique that I was changed by the experience. Joe, Lynn, Norman, and Lenai each left impressions on my being that would last my entire life. Israel was no different, for in Ze'ev Silverman I had such a person.

Ze'ev taught the Anatomy courses at MSIH, and an elective course in Ethics. Originally from Baltimore, Maryland, he was a cellular neuroscientist by training whose claim to fame was studying under the famous anatomist, Richard Snell. He was also an Orthodox Jew. He wore a black felt kippa and lived a life of strict adherence to the letter, and spirit, of the Jewish Law.

He had made *aliyah* to Israel decades before as a young man. *Aliyah* is the Hebrew term for the act of Jewish immigration to Israel. Translated 'ascent', it reflects how one always goes up to Jerusalem, both physically and spiritually. In making *aliyah*, Ze'ev left the ease of American life for the heavy emotional burden of life in Israel. His existence was responsively modest, living with his wife and three children in a small one story townhouse.

Ze'ev had one simple, yet fundamentally attractive quality: he listened. A heated discussion between two or three people is seldom linear. It is circular with tangents flaring off like meteors spit out of their orbit because neither side listens to the other. They merely contemplate their next point. Not so with Ze'ev, who moved conversations forward with focused listening, digesting each statement before offering a cogent response that was reactionary, not obligatory. He didn't push his own agenda. Where I saw this trait come alive was at Ze'ev's quite famous Shabbat dinners.

The Jewish week is built around the Shabbat. It begins Friday at sundown and ends Saturday at sundown. Within those 24 hours, the observant Jew is forbidden to do any work. This includes menial tasks such as flipping a light-switch or tearing off a piece of toilet paper. As a result, the entire country takes a rest. No public transportation operates. Gates are locked and shades drawn on all manners of business. Only those catering specifically to the expatriate, or the most secular Jew, open their doors on Shabbat. A general quiet takes over each city and town.

Friday night dinner is spent at home with family and friends. Prayers are said and sung and wine is poured, all with great ritual. Ze'ev's habit was to invite MSIH students over each week for this meal, and these invitations were highly sought after amongst the student body. On our fourth Saturday back in Israel, Shelley and I would be spending Shabbat dinner in Ze'ev's home.

Ze'ev's house was in the same neighborhood as our old apartment on Ayala Street. The area wasn't pleasant aesthetically, being mostly communist block apartment shells, but to us it was warmly familiar. Waiting for dusk to come, we walked around to see and remember the place we first lived as a married couple.

We passed the *gesher* (bridge), so named for a pedestrian overpass leading from Ze'ev's housing complex to a nearby strip mall. This small outpost of shops has everything needed to sustain life: post office, bakery, flower shop, supermarket, bank, and of course a shwarma stand. It made life incredibly convenient for Shelley and me during medical school.

From there we turned up into the central neighborhood park. A sprawling, hilly expanse in the middle of the city, it serves as a refuge for the largest ethnic population in Beer Sheva, the Russians. We heard no Hebrew spoken while walking through. Russian men played chess on benches and tables throughout the park, usually in large groups as though watching a soccer match. Other groups of men walked with hands behind their backs enjoying the setting afternoon sun.

There were other people groups huddled together on blankets cooking out or playing with their children. Their olive skin told me they were Sephardic in background. In Jewish culture, and in Israeli society, a distinction is made between the Ashkenazi and Sephardic ethnicities. The Ashkenazi Jews came out of Western and Eastern Europe, as well as Russia and the lesser parts of the old U.S.S.R. They hold Israel's cultural, historical, and economic power.

The Sephardic Jews, by definition, originated from Spain, but the reference includes those from historically Muslim countries in North Africa and the Middle East: Morocco, Tunisia, Yemen, Iraq, and Iran. What these Jews lack in social power, they make up for in cultural influence through a lively and laid back approach to life, religion, and especially food. Most of the families we saw in the park were Moroccan.

We finally came to Ze'ev's home once night had fallen. We weren't given a time to arrive. Shabbat dinner starts after sun down, so we showed up then. Rise, Ze'ev's wife, greeted us warmly at the door, as did their three young daughters. Ze'ev was on the couch talking with the other evening guests, two younger medical students from my program.

"How are you, Doctor Neese?" He asked, pulling himself up off the couch.

"Still another month to get that title," I replied, "but I'm almost there. Can you believe it?"

"The days are long, but the years go by fast. Congratulations!" His voice inflections undulated in a definitive way, as though remnants of a stutter long since educated out of him.

After conversing on the couch, Ze'ev invited everyone to the table.

"Rise and I hope you enjoy dinner tonight," he proclaimed. "Today, we welcome the Shabbat. We celebrate this day as the day God rested from his creation."

Ze'ev is a thin man with a runner's frame, though he doesn't exercise at all. His lips are thick and the upper half drifted up, resting his mouth in an open position leaving his two front teeth exposed. He had been to *shul*, the local Synagogue, for Friday prayers and was dressed in the uniform of the Orthodox Jew: black felt kippa, white button down shirt, black slacks, and black leather shoes.

This uniform alone made Judaism intimidating to me. Orthodox Jews seem recluse in their religiosity and their unyielding regulations make it hard for an outsider to enter and explore their world. Despite the Jewish roots of Christianity, I found it difficult to identify common ground. Shelley and I once met an Orthodox Jew in Safed, a city in northern Israel, who refused even to make eye contact with her. How could I relate to that?

Ze'ev made Orthodox Judaism approachable. Through him I could ask questions and understand their perspective. I could learn their ways, which I soon held in high regard. Ze'ev not only looked Shelley in the eye, he took a keen interest in her career and personal life story.

"In general, Jews celebrate by eating." Ze'ev continued. "Perhaps you've noticed the theme of every Jewish holiday is the same: Somebody wanted to kill us, we survived, let's eat! So, let us eat indeed, but first, we wash our hands."

This was the first order of ceremony for the night. Everyone lined up at the sink and filled a special two-handled jar with water. Their jar happened to be a gift from Shelley and me when we left Israel the last time. I jokingly noted to Rise how beautiful the jar was. She smiled, but she could not speak because she'd already washed her hands. She would have to wait for the cutting of the challah bread to speak another sound.

I washed with two pours of water over one hand, and two pours of water over the other. Under my breath I said the Hebrew prayer that accompanied this ritual, "*Baruch atah Adonai Elohaynu melech ha-olam, asher kid'shanu b'mitzvotav, v'tzivanu al n'tilat yadayim.*"[2] A religious classmate had taught me that prayer a few years before. I was happy to intimately participate in this ceremony.

Around the table there was silence, but there was also activity. Hand gestures, games with silverware, these were the ways children kept silent. It rubbed off on the adults as well as Ze'ev's young daughter, Abigail, and I played a childish game with our forks.

With everyone now at the table, Ze'ev removed the cover from the braided challah bread. He placed the blade of his knife against the bread, and then recited the following prayer, "*Baruch atah Adonai Elohaynu melech ha-olam, ha-motzi lechem min ha-aretz. Amen.*"[3] He cut the bread and tongues were unbound. Chatter began in earnest as the challah bread was passed around the table.

Since the day I had left Israel for my fourth year, I had longed to be in this moment. I was keenly aware of my contentment as I sat listening and watching the interaction around the table. Our conversation threaded from one topic to another, pushed

---

2 Blessed are You, Lord, our God, King of the Universe who sanctifies us with his commandments, and commands us concerning washing of hands.

3 Blessed are You, Lord, our God, King of the Universe who brings forth bread from the earth. Amen.

forward with Ze'ev's inconspicuous guidance. Aside from his aforementioned qualities in conversation, Ze'ev was also very smart and well read outside his own scientific specialty. He propagated any topic with aptitude.

Ze'ev then asked me about my plans after graduation.

"I've decided to do Family Medicine," I said. "It was a stressful decision. I was on the verge of choosing Psychiatry."

"You definitely live in your head, don't you?"

"I guess there's no changing that now. To be honest, Ze'ev, medicine is a struggle for me. I love the interaction with patients, and I'm observant, but I get bogged down by the details of the machine, if you know what I mean."

"I'm an anatomist, I know what you mean."

"Psychiatry seemed free flowing, more focused on the narrative and that fits my brain a lot better."

"Why Family Medicine then?"

"In the end, I couldn't relegate myself to one aspect of a patient's life. Actually, I couldn't relegate my life to one aspect of medicine. That never appealed to me. Family Medicine lets you be a jack of all trades, a master of none. That fits me and I have a peace about going into it."

"Everything in life is a compromise. I thought about doing medicine, but I didn't want to make life and death decisions on people. I wonder at times if I would have enjoyed medicine, but that's the give and take. There's an old Yiddish proverb that says 'Man plans and God laughs.' We always want control, but it's not ours to have. The decision you made will be the right one."

Ze'ev's words gave me comfort. I valued his guidance and held it close. Even spiritually I respected him deeply, though his religion was not my own. I knew he was a man who earnestly sought after God. In fact, I had met few in my life as honest in their faith as Ze'ev Silverman. His word I could trust.

When dessert and coffee were done, Rise distributed prayer books. Each book was different, but all were hawked from some or another Jewish wedding. The books had Hebrew script and an English translation.

Hebrew, like Arabic, is a Semitic language without any semblance to Latin. While I could speak Hebrew well, reading it was exceedingly difficult. It is written in block form, each letter disconnected from the other and without vowels. The text flows from right to left, which means that pages of a book or magazine turn 'backwards', only adding to the frustration. I did my best to follow along during the prayers, but failure was imminent and repetitive. I soon felt Abigail's gentle nudge. She kindly advanced my pages when necessary so that I could feign participation.

After dinner we left the Silverman house and walked off hand in hand into a cool Beer Sheva. The streets were quiet because of the Shabbat, with only the occasional white Taxi slowing down to offer us a ride. The last thing on earth we wanted was to arrive home faster. We savored this moment, reliving the evening's conversations, sharing observations we couldn't express at the table, and thinking about how far we had come since our first Shabbat dinner. What was once so strange now seemed familiar, and with a wholeness that came from sharing an intimate experience with people we hold dear. The walk home in the afterglow of such a special evening was the perfect cool down to a natural high, and came in at #6 on my LOTIL.

As we entered the main drag leading to our hotel, I turned to Shelley and asked, "Have you ever heard the saying, 'When a wise person dies, it is like a library was burned down'?"

"Yeah. Why?"

"I'm gonna say that about Ze'ev if I ever get that news." Shelley nodded in agreement.

I had another thought that I didn't share with her as we walked. I knew that I would also weep on that day, no matter how old or how removed I was from Israel and those Shabbat dinners around Ze'ev's table. In him, I saw a way of right living that I could model myself after. So every moment in the same room with him was total absorption, gathering pearls of wisdom and tucking them into a hidden place in my heart. To lose Ze'ev would be much more than a library to me.

Soda Popinski and the Cardiac Cocktail

I was in the final stretch of my fourth year. At this point, none of us really cared about studying, or participating in our rotations. These last weeks were formalities to graduate. We had already matched into our specialties, and I knew I'd be spending the next three years specializing in Family Medicine at the University of Virginia in Charlottesville, Virginia. Shelley and I would be together, under one roof, in our very own home. Lord willing, we would begin to expand our family as well.

Even though my eyes were now gazing squarely on the future, I was reflective about what I had just experienced in my fourth year. I wasn't ready for complete independence as a doctor. Internship and residency would transform that part of me. Nevertheless, I wasn't the same person as when I started this year. What had changed? I still wasn't sure. There was one more experience left that would clarify the difference my fourth year had made. It came in the most gruesome place.

Though never a "procedure hound", I take a morbid enjoyment in phlebotomy. Blood sticks, intravenous lines, central lines, and epidurals were all things I would try while rotating through Anesthesiology.

Dr. Fedorov, the attending physician in charge of my rotation, was a Russian doctor. He immigrated to Israel as an adult, already a specialized physician. Russian immigrants are often highly educated professionals, engineers, and doctors back home. Many are forced to work as cleaners and janitors because there is no room for their skills in Israel.

I met Fedorov in the operating theater's staff lounge at 6:45 AM on the dot. He stood by a table, sucking on a thin, dark brown cigarette. He was setting down his coffee and a saucer of boiled eggs, tomato slices, and a small tub of hummus.

"What is the sequence for rapid intubation of a patient?" So much for good mornings, this was Fedorov's greeting to me. It was as unpleasant as the smoke that wafted out of his mouth with each word. I squeezed my eyes and mouth shut to avoid inhaling or absorbing the smoke.

"I know you use Etomidate and Succinylcholine." I fanned my hand across my face to clear the air. "I think Etomidate is the first step." Any hints of my discomfort were lost on Dr. Fedorov.

Equally lost on him was the pathetic answer I had thrown out. He quickly answered his own question and went through, step-by-step, the procedure for rapid sequence intubation. This mini-lecture ended with another question that stumped me. Clearly, I was trapped in the middle of a good old fashioned pimp session. Getting pimped is medical student slang for being charged a litany of questions by your superior, requiring medical knowledge you probably don't have. You might get lucky, but answering correctly only promises a more difficult question.

I used a brilliant subversion tactic to squirm my way out of this difficult situation. While not fast on the draw with answers, I can always think of a question. In fact, I live with a million questions in my mind, like bullets in a gun magazine, just waiting for the chance to get out. By answering Dr. Fedorov with equally thought provoking questions, I turned the pimp session on its head. For the next quarter of an hour I listened intently as he discussed with great enthusiasm the nuances of putting a patient to sleep.

In the middle of Fedorov's monologue, his left eye wandered off as though completely disconnected from his forward gaze. I followed the drifting eye, wondering what could be causing such a distraction, but quickly caught myself, realizing he was not in control of that wandering eye. With all my might, I kept focus on his right eye, the good eye, even as the other one drifted in and out. I feared his embarrassment of the pathologic eyeball.

Fedorov, however, was not embarrassed easily. His flat facial expressions, a common trait amongst the Russian population, made it hard to decipher what emotions he possessed. He seemed to me a living, breathing version of Soda Popinski, a character known to all who played Mike Tyson's Punch-Out on Nintendo. Picture a muscular Russian with pink skin and a curly moustache. Fedorov wore his green surgical scrubs tight and he never changed out of his pointy, black leather dress shoes.

I was able to end the pimp session outright by asking him about his life back in Russia. This was another trick I had in my repertoire. It played on the fact that everybody in the human race enjoys talking about themselves. It is the most interesting thing to each of us. Even for Dr. Fedorov.

He said he fought for the Russian Army in the Russian-Afghan war by transporting injured soldiers from Kabul to Moscow or St. Petersburg. Patients were anesthetized under his care in two fully functioning surgical theaters on board cargo planes. I asked him about the war itself, which had received much attention leading up to the United States' war in Afghanistan.

"We fought only to beat the Americans," he said. "To show strength, nothing else. But it was a guerilla war, and you can never win a guerilla war. The guerillas always win."

We each grabbed a surgical mask and entered the operating theater. The patient on the table, Avner Levin, was a morbidly obese taxi driver in Beer Sheva. A smoker since he was an 18 year old foot soldier in the Army, the hardened arteries feeding oxygen to his heart were about to be rerouted. A tech was just removing the knitted blue kippa from his head.

Avner was my first chance to place a central venous line, a rare opportunity for any medical student. Needles and large bore catheters are pushed into huge veins dumping straight into the heart. There are significant risks, like puncturing a lung or hitting a major artery by mistake. Things can go bad, fast.

Following Fedorov's guiding hand and verbal direction I tried three times to hit the Internal Jugular, a large vein in the neck. Unfortunately for Avner, his neck was the size of a small tire, warping the key landmarks to central line placement. I was pushing the needle in blind.

My psyche was redeemed when Fedorov also failed at placing the line. A third party came in and was finally successful. Though I failed at the line placement, I was excited to watch the rest of this surgery. I had never seen an open heart procedure.

The room was functioning at a very high state, each person moving with purpose. Whether it was the nurse counting out cold steel instruments on a waist high movable tray, techs calibrating the pumps that would soon be rerouting and oxygenating Avner's blood, or Fedorov preparing his magic potions that would ensure Avner didn't feel or remember a thing, all occurred as a well-rehearsed dance.

Fedorov began speaking to Avner about the procedure at the same time a nurse began cleaning off his chest.

"Friend, are you ready for this?"

"Of course I'm not ready. Look at this. My chest is about to be opened!"

"You sound just like the last guy. He lived, just so you know."

"Let's get on with this thing, better to get it over with."

"Everything will be alright, my friend." Fedorov drew up a thick white solution called propofol and pushed it through his I.V. line. "Good night and good luck." Fedorov's curly mustache, pink skin, the wandering eye, and his thick Russian accent must have been quite a sight to Avner Levin, the Beer Sheva cabbie. Avner tried to respond to the salutation, but was snoring before he completed a sentence in reply.

My view at the end of the table was perfect for this operation. So often surgeries are difficult to watch because the organs are deep in a body cavity, and you're stuck behind the surgeon.

You can prop up onto a stool, but standing on your toes and leaning over becomes tedious as minutes drag on into hours. As the surgeon sawed open Avner's chest and opened the cardiac cavity, the beating heart was elevated as though presenting it at a banquet feast. I was staring right at it.

The heart throbbed, its chambers bulging out like translucent fish cheeks, thin except for the much thicker walls of muscle driving each beat. It didn't squirm or wiggle like a fish out of water. In fact, even sitting outside the chest cavity it was functioning in its normal capacity, its only manifestation of stress the increased rate of its beat. This quickening was soon calmed when a surgical assistant poured sterile ice into the cardiac cavity. The surgeon then went to work at rerouting the blood flow.

He placed tubes into the entrance and exit points of the heart so that Avner's blood was securely bypassing the heart, dumping carbon dioxide and picking up oxygen in the machine sitting five feet from his body. This allowed the rest of his body to continue its normal functioning. The heart was then brought to a complete stop with an injection of potassium chloride.

Avner had been placed up on the blocks so to speak, no different than an old car getting a new transmission. His life was, at the moment, utterly dependent on the competency and knowledge of this medical team, whose leader finally entered the surgical suite. He was a short man, as wide as he was tall. He gowned up with his hands dripping water from the same penitent position as the previous surgeon. This was Dr. Simmerman, the most senior surgeon at Soroka Medical Center, the top of a ferocious surgical hierarchy. Some said he was the highest paid physician in all of Israel. With precision incongruent to his awkward frame, he rerouted the coronary arteries, bypassing fatty clots that were threatening Avner's life.

Simmerman's dexterity was otherworldly. I stared at his hands that so fluidly pulled sutures through, tying them down so quickly I could scarcely tell what hand was doing what. Their knowing movements never hesitated, not once. When his hand wasn't moving, it sat perfectly still without any hint of natural tremor, no finger tapped in indecision, no fist curled up in frustration, they didn't even wiggle in anticipation. Every move was purposeful, as if choreographed down to the last minutia of movement.

My entire time in medical school, I never looked at a surgeon's hands without an overwhelming sense of guilt and jealousy. This had little to do with the act of surgery itself. God had not given me such dexterity, or a mind so briskly functioning as to ever become a surgeon. It was actually that surgeons were so competent at their work, so skilled that confidence exuded even from their finger tips. The careful choreography was simply a manifestation of exceeding confidence. I had always lacked this confidence because I did not yet have the competence. That explained the jealousy.

The guilt came because what I saw of medicine, whose epitome I gazed upon in that surgical theatre, did not come natural to me. Breaking down the human being, with whom I'd always felt an emotional attraction, into machine parts to be cut out, revamped, re-routed, suppressed, cajoled, or otherwise tinkered with, did not suit me. I struggled with this from the first lecture in medical school and at every stage thereafter. During my first clinical experiences in third year, each patient became an elevated white blood cell count or a fractured humerus or a stomach cancer. Their names, their personal story, and their heritage took a back seat to the necessities of medical practice.

Where did I fit into this puzzle? Being an intimate part of a patient's unfolding life story seemed in painful conflict to the demands of modern medicine, which eschewed the relationship for the biomechanics of pathophysiology and pharmacology. I could fit the clinical pieces together, but did I want to? What price was I willing to pay to pursue that end? These questions floated like a permanent road sign I passed every day walking to the hospital.

Standing at Avner's feet with his stilled heart resting in his chest cavity, and with Dr. Simmerman's glorious hands working out a medical miracle, I felt no guilt, nor did I hold an ounce of jealousy. The biomechanics of medicine were important, but my fourth year of medical school made me understand that lab values, numbers, statistics, and even the disease process itself were not a complete picture of a patient's health and well being. I saw this in the forgiveness after Mrs. Cohen's disimpaction, which came about only after an honest exchange between us. I saw it in Maria's mournful state and the Subway Evangelist's joyful rebirth. Their personal stories spoke volumes about their physical well being. I saw it in Lynn and Norman Morrison who made me a part of their family, adopting me into a Native American tribe that my people have oppressed for hundreds of years. That happened because of a relationship.

I also saw the fragility of medicine in the deaths I experienced, some with my eyes, some with my own bare hands. Healing is a mystery beyond the power of medical knowledge, regardless of the doctor or surgeon. As impressive as Simmerman was in that operating theater, his sutures only approximated tissues, they didn't re-seal them. Man can saw, cut, and destroy, but only the body can re-seal, grow, and heal. Without this power, which cannot be seen or measured, medicine in all its forms is useless and futile.

In Avner, I saw a book with many chapters. The first chapter started well before his first breath, and the last chapters would continue long after today's events, even if Dr. Simmerman failed to revive the heart he had stilled. Today was just a moment in that book, this problem just one event in the course of Avner's life. It hardly summed up all there was to know of him, nor did it reveal what brought him here, or how he would handle life from here on. Someone had to read his book. Some physician had to know his story, because that story mattered to Avner's health and his quality of life. It mattered in how he would heal and rehabilitate after the surgeons stitched him back up.

That somebody, in a proverbial sense, was me.

I could stand tall in front of those surgeons, not because of my competence in medicine, which was still in its infancy, but because I had a place in medicine. A place that would make a difference in the life of a patient like Avner, and that would not leave me bitter that I had sold my soul to chase what other people, or the system, said I must follow. It was a path of relationships, a back and forth of experience with patients over a period of time. If this space wasn't in the surgical theatre, or even the hospital floor, icons of what it means to be a doctor, it was still a space that matters to each and every patient, and even to the field of medicine.

Avner's coronary arteries were successfully re-routed and his chest wall was re-approximated. It would be quite painful every time he so much as coughed, until the fibers of those tissues and bones wove themselves back together. For now, though, he would wake up happy to know his life did not come to an abrupt end there on the operating table.

On my way out I grabbed Avner's medical chart. The first page was a sheet of labels with his name, date of birth, and the like. I peeled one off and slapped it over my watch so I'd remember to visit him later that day. I had a few questions I wanted to ask him. It's what I do.

Acknowledgments

This book contains events and conversations from my fourth year of medical school. I have been truthful in this text and as accurate as my memory and the narrative would allow. When necessary, and including every patient, a character's real name has been changed to protect their identity.

I'd like to thank Christina Ankeney, the mother of a household of small children and a master of the English language, who turned this manuscript into a true narrative. To Joan Tapper, a professional editor, who gently cut away the chaff and strengthened the text.

My classmate, Geoff Ankeney, was the first to lay eyes on this manuscript, to which he responded, "It actually doesn't suck." These words kept the dream alive! Lynn Aucoin and David Carnahan gave a critical eye to this work. Melanie Barfield, a talented graphic artist, captured the essence of the book with her cover design. I am grateful to each of them for their time and assistance on this project.

Profound thanks to the Medical School for International Health. To Carmi Margolis and Richard Deckelbaum, who brought something to life without precedent, a path of truly global and cross cultural medical education. Their vision has given wings to people like me. The program office at Columbia University, led by Pamela Cooper and Alice Mahoney, who have encouraged me since the day I interviewed in 1999. And to professors such as Shimon Glick, Lehaim Naggan, and Mick Alkan, their legacy permeates every patient encounter in this book.

To my wife, Shelley, you've been my consultant, editor, encourager, and partner. Your love reaches my inmost being, where it waters the seeds of all my hopes and dreams. That is where I hold you, now and forever, my Righteous Gentile. I love you.

Finally, I give thanks to God, for He is the beginning and end of all things.